Barcode →

Photographs on the preceding pages by Lars Tunbjörk. Tunbjörk, a freelance photographer working out of Stockholm, has photographed offices around the world. These off-beat images catch the office after hours—or at least unawares.

*on the job*

# on the job:
# design and the american office

**Donald Albrecht and
Chrysanthe B. Broikos, editors**

**Princeton Architectural Press**
New York, New York

**National Building Museum**
Washington, D.C.

This book is published in conjunction with the exhibition
*On the Job: Design and the American Office*, presented at the
National Building Museum, Washington, D.C., November 18,
2000–June 24, 2001.

**Co-curators:** Donald Albrecht and Chrysanthe B. Broikos
**Editor:** Natalie Shivers
**Designer:** Pentagram

**Major funding for the catalog and exhibition is provided by:**

## Gensler

HAWORTH

HermanMiller

## McGraw-Hill Construction Information Group

F.W.DODGE  ARCHITECTURAL RECORD  Sweet's Group  ENR  Design•Build

## Milliken Foundation

Steelcase

**Additional funding is provided by:**

Armstrong World Industries, James G. Davis Construction
Corporation, M. Arthur Gensler Jr., FAIA, FIIDA, RIBA, Interface,
Wilsonart International, and Ai, Cushman & Wakefield,
Edward Fields, Johnson Controls, Hines, RTKL Associates, Teknion

Davis·Carter·Scott, Fixtures Furniture, GHT Limited Consulting
Engineers, Harter, Mannington, Shaw Contract Group, Skidmore,
Owings & Merrill, Truland Foundation

Corporate Interiors Publishing, CUH2A, Design Collective
Incorporated, Fortune Contract, Freestate Electrical Construction
Company, Gwathmey Siegel & Associates Architects,
International Interior Design Association, Lehman-Smith +
McLeish, OP·X, Tate Access Floors, Tri-State Drywall,
Westland Printers, Hickok Warner Fox Architects, and
Walter A. Hunt, Jr., AIA & Judith T. Hunt

**Published by**
Princeton Architectural Press
37 East 7th Street
New York, New York 10003
www.papress.com

and

National Building Museum
401 F Street, N.W.
Washington, D.C. 20001
www.nbm.org

**Project editor:** Beth Harrison
**Consulting editor:** Natalie Shivers
**Book design:** J. Abbott Miller and Roy Brooks, Pentagram
**Information graphics:** Alicia Yin Cheng

Special thanks to Ann Alter, Amanda Atkins, Eugenia Bell,
Jan Cigliano, Jane Garvie, Caroline Green, Mia Ihara,
Clare Jacobson, Leslie Ann Kent, Mark Lamster, Anne Nitschke,
Lottchen Shivers, Jennifer Thompson, and Deb Wood of
Princeton Architectural Press
—Kevin C. Lippert, Publisher

For a free catalog of other books published by Princeton
Architectural Press, call toll free 1.800.722.6657.

**Library of Congress Cataloging-in-Publication Data**
On the job : design and the American office /
Donald Albrecht and Chrysanthe B. Broikos, editors.
p. cm.
Catalog of an exhibition held at the National Building Museum.
Includes bibliographical references.
ISBN 1-56898-241-0 (alk. paper)
1. Office decoration—United States—History—
20th century—Exhibitions. 2. Interior decoration—
Human factors—Exhibitions. 3. Interior architecture—
United States—Exhibitions. I. Albrecht, Donald. II.
Broikos, Chrysanthe B. III. National Building Museum (U.S.)
NK2195.04 05 2000
725'.23'0973074753—dc21
00-009563

Front and back cover: Lobby and typical office floor, Union Carbide
Building, 1960; New York, New York; Architect: Skidmore, Owings
& Merrill; Photographer: Ezra Stoller © Esto. All right reserved.

# contents

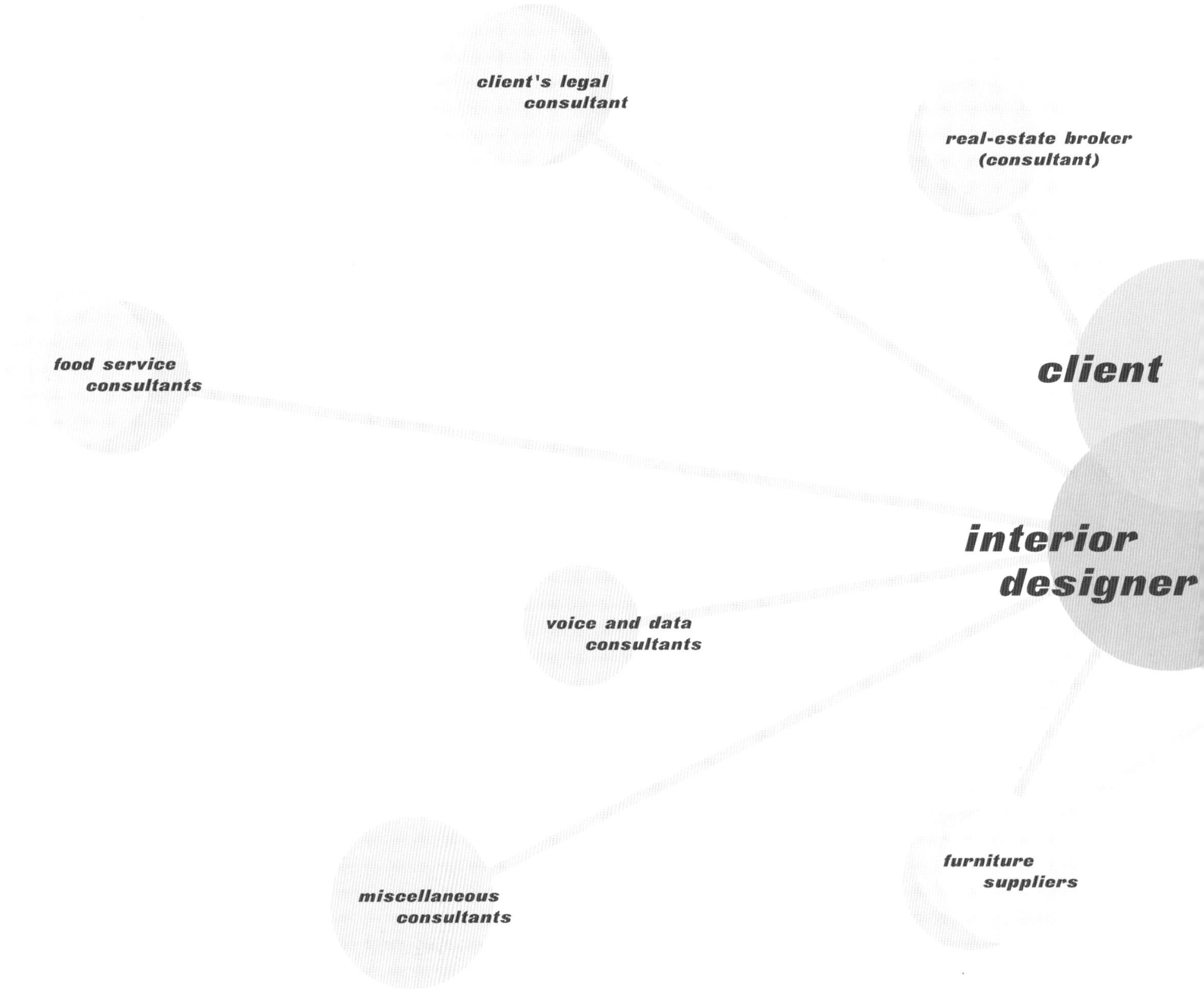

client's legal
consultant

real-estate broker
(consultant)

food service
consultants

client

interior
designer

voice and data
consultants

furniture
suppliers

miscellaneous
consultants

Source: *Office Planning
and Design Desk Reference*
(1992, John Wiley & Sons)
edited by James E. Rappoport,
Robert F. Cushman, and
Karen Daroff.

**building code
permit authority**

**project engineering**

**architect**

**building security
consultant**

**construction manager/
contractor**

**miscellaneous
consultants**

**subcontractors
and suppliers**

**site civil engineering
consultants**

**Great Hall of the Pension Building (now National Building Museum),** c.1963; Washington, D.C.; Architect: Montgomery C. Meigs; National Building Museum Collection

Completed in 1887, the Museum's home was originally a federal office building where government workers processed the pension benefits of Civil War veterans. The Great Hall was designed to host inaugural balls but was converted into office space as early as the 1920s and outfitted with office partitions and fluorescent lights around 1960.

# *foreword*

Susan Henshaw Jones

The office—whether downtown, in a suburban office park, or at home—is the place where the majority of Americans spend the majority of their day. While some 60 percent of us hold desk jobs, we are no longer tied to the same desk for our entire careers. New language already reflects the fluidity and mobility of this postindustrial, white-collar world; today's office is a somewhat arbitrary, if not temporary, "workplace," and the desk has been replaced by a "workstation."

The office as a place, however, is not disappearing, but merely transforming itself, as it has always done. *On the Job: Design and the American Office* examines the workplace at the very moment the office is making a resurgence, retooling itself to be a place of creative interaction. Where did the modern office model come from? How has it been understood? And where is it going? This catalog and the corresponding exhibition focus not only on the literal, physical changes in the American office but

also on the cultural shifts that have accompanied these transformations.

A private, nonprofit educational institution, the National Building Museum explores the what, who, how, and why of American building through exhibitions, publications, and programs. The Museum's historic home originally housed the U.S. Pension Bureau and was later occupied by many other government agencies. With the opening of *On the Job*, these offices-turned-galleries are again home to an array of office environments.

Offices—indeed, commercial interiors of all types—are often underutilized laboratories for the investigation of the many connections between the way we build and the way we live, or, in this case, the way we work. Our offices indicate—subtly and not so subtly—status, hierarchy, and what types of work are most valued. In the past, the size of your office or whether your desk was wood or metal reflected your place within an organization. Today, a more precise measure of whether you're on the fast track is the level of technology available. Do you have the best or newest computer? The latest gadget or high-tech office toy? Change often comes to the office first, in the name of efficiency, productivity, or profits. Thanks to professional designers, new solutions come with creativity and style.

Many people and organizations contributed to *On the Job: Design and the American Office,* and we are indebted to them all for participating. Special thanks are due to M. Arthur Gensler Jr., vice chair of the Museum's Board of Trustees and the founder and principal of Gensler Architecture, Design & Planning Worldwide. Gensler's lead gift to the Museum was pivotal, and Art played a key role amassing the necessary support for this project. Likewise, Art's firm has been a major force in developing the architecture of the workplace; his office received the 2000 Architecture Firm Award from the American Institute of Architects. No one is more

qualified to provide the preface to *On the Job* than Art, and I thank him for his unwavering dedication.

The idea for this project actually originated through Art's firm during a conversation I had with Diane Hoskins, managing principal in Gensler's Washington, D.C., office. The International Interior Design Association (IIDA) also provided important early leadership, funding the initial exhibition proposal and opening countless doors.

Significant funding has been provided by Gensler Architecture, Design & Planning Worldwide, M. Arthur Gensler Jr., Haworth, Herman Miller, McGraw-Hill Construction Information Group, Milliken Foundation, and Steelcase, as well as Armstrong World Industries, James G. Davis Construction Corporation, Interface, and Wilsonart International.

My thanks, as well, to co-curators and catalog editors Donald Albrecht and Chrysanthe B. Broikos for bringing the American office into focus. This

work, the third National Building Museum catalog designed by Pentagram's J. Abbott Miller, offers a unique, interdisciplinary perspective on the place where most of us spend our waking hours.

Susan Henshaw Jones is president of the National Building Museum.

# *preface*

## *a personal history of the workplace revolution*

M. Arthur Gensler Jr., FAIA, FIIDA, RIBA

Let me begin by saluting the National Building Museum and its sponsors for mounting this exhibition, and Princeton Architectural Press for publishing this handsome book on the settings that people experience on a near-daily basis over their working lives. All this is something of a coming of age for the workplace as a cultural phenomenon. This isn't home we're talking about, but for most working adults it comes pretty close.

My colleagues in this enterprise, historians and journalists alike, have ably covered the history of the workplace over the last century. What I'd like to provide here is a coda—an account of the last third of this history by a practicing architect and workplace specialist who experienced it in real time.

I started my firm in 1965, a time when offices (as we called them then) were still mostly laid out on graph paper by office managers in back rooms. Their attitude was strictly utilitarian: Fit them in. Not many companies back then thought of their offices as a strategic resource, but a growing number were headed steadily in that direction. What were their concerns? Here's a sampling from our projects in the 1970s:

"Enhance communication between departments."

"Achieve a higher level of flexibility."

"Reduce office sizes."

"Focus on client service."

"Support long-range business goals."

In terms of technology, this was the decade when office landscaping (or cubicles, as we call them today) was introduced, along with electromagnetic typewriters (the first step toward word processing), Xerox copiers, and rudimentary fax machines.

Things really started to change in the 1980s. Companies were more aware of their specific functional needs, but they also saw that growth and change brought "churn." That could mean ongoing turmoil in the workplace unless it were managed correctly; we developed universal planning in this decade to cope with it. Companies also began to sever the relationship between space and status ("Express rank by furniture and finishes, not by size"). This was the decade, too, when office automation—standalone word processors, first, and then the ubiquitous personal computer—appeared.

People associate the 1980s with trophy office towers designed to celebrate the corporate ego. Yet this decade also saw the emergence of the first generation of upstarts—companies like Apple Computer that helped shift the center of high-tech gravity from Armonk and Boston to Silicon Valley. What were their concerns?

"Reinforce our corporate culture."

"Give us an informal working environment."

"Give us spaces that users can define."

"Give us a collaborative workplace that sparks creativity and speeds time to market."

People remember (and pillory) the 1980s for their extravagance, but many seeds of the now-ongoing workplace revolution were planted in that enterprising decade.

The 1990s built on this theme and added some ideas of its own. The U.S. recession of the early 1990s influenced the evolving workplace, too. We found Apple, for example, asking us to "consolidate groups that are now spread across the country" and "invest simple materials with visual energy" (i.e., "flash without cash"). Despite the sputtering economy, the concerns of the first half of the 1990s were remarkably forward-looking:

"Help us respond faster to changing markets and technology."

"Give us an environmentally responsive building."

"Challenge preconceived notions of the successful workplace."

"Help people escape from corporate structure, work out of the box."

"Enhance employee productivity."

"Create an environment where people can work in teams."

"Make us a high-performance, on-line workplace—quick and cheap."

"Eliminate hierarchies! Blur the boundaries! Teams rule!"

America's mid-1990s economic recovery coincided with its decisive shift into the current bandwidth era, when a series of innovations suddenly made economic sense and spurred a full-scale rethinking of how we work and how we do business. That rethink has taken on greater urgency as more and more of the economy hits Web speed.

Bandwidth brought CEOs back into the workplace picture after a considerable absence. They followed the lead of their human resources people, who were the first to notice that a well-designed workplace can improve employees' performance. CEOs were our clients in the 1960s and 1970s, but they were supplanted by facilities managers in the 1980s. Early on, these property professionals assured us that they could speak for CEOs and users alike. Today, they are valued allies in the building process, but the CEOs and the users both speak for themselves.

The best evidence for the impact of a well-designed workplace on human performance comes from Colorado's Rocky Mountain Institute. Its case studies of "green" office buildings and factories document consistent productivity gains of 2 to 6 percent attributable to better lighting, improved air quality, and greater thermal comfort. Productivity is a big deal because the cost of labor dwarfs every other cost. Workplace measures that result in gains of this order can pay for themselves quickly.

Bandwidth accelerates everything. The expression "moving at Web speed" is no joke. Consider this U.K. telecom company: A protected monopoly, it was forced by deregulation to shift from work "in series," passed from one department to another, to work "in parallel," carried out by teams that form and disband constantly. It sells 4,500 different, mostly Internet-focused products, many with life cycles of six months or less, so it has aligned its workplace with its bandwidth. Its Intranet is its glue, allowing its workforce to book space on demand, store and retrieve team documents, communicate with their teams, access a variety of services, and learn at a distance. Its buildings serve as hubs; people go there to meet others and work, talk, or train together face to face. For most teams, the ratio of people to desks is four to one.

Why is this strategic? Let's look at what it has accomplished for the company:

A stable workforce of 130,000 people
(although its revenues have tripled)

A $1.6 billion savings
(largely due to much higher building utilization)

Faster and faster time to market
(a key measure of success in the bandwidth era).

All this efficiency is achieved with work settings that are striking for their quality and amenity. This is, in fact, a key part of the tradeoff companies are making now with their workforce. Consider the Los Angeles regional headquarters of a global consulting firm. The old model, connecting space with status, is out the window. The new model provides a range of spaces that reflect how people really work.

These settings are tailor-made for the activities they support, but their allocation reflects patterns of actual use. Again, bandwidth glues this together, enabling people to book ahead for the space they need.

The bandwidth era gave some people the idea that "place" might be superfluous. The retail sector is a good example: Many predicted that e-commerce would wipe out bricks-and-mortar retail, but it hasn't happened. The market leaders have pursued a "clicks-and-mortar" strategy that plays their Web presence off their stores, and vice versa.

One of our current workplace clients actually launched its business with the goal of being a "virtual company." Because they conduct clinical trials, organizing as an electronic network of home-based knowledge workers made initial sense. In time, though, their lack of "place" proved a drag on growth. They needed places where they could get together on a regional basis—a corporate hearth.

Clearly, place matters. This is especially true when companies merge or consolidate. As network expert Karen Stephenson, management professor at the University of California, Los Angeles, puts it, "The physical settings of newly merged organizations can help or hinder the process of establishing trust among key individuals and joining networks. Propinquity—physical closeness—is critical to breaking down the normal barriers between 'tribes' like experts and innovators. In the distant past, networks began as face-to-face encounters and conversations. We still carry that legacy with us today."[1]

If you think about how much money is at stake in a merger, the fact that its success is riding on workplace issues underscores the economic importance of workplace design. It's not really about efficiency—that's almost a given in the new economy. Today's fast companies are focused on productivity, time to market, and the leverage they can get from merging or consolidating. Their goal is to generate wealth from the strategic elements of their business, and that's really what workplace designers do, too.

One of my colleagues at Gensler calls the workplace "connective tissue." Place, people, work processes, and technology are the strategic elements of a business, the engine that—when all pistons are firing—drives our economy. Our own practice reflects this. We engage our clients now as they're framing their business plans, and then partner with them across the full strategic cycle. Yet that was always implicit in our client relationships. Organizational issues, real-estate strategies, program and facilities management responsibilities—all of these are part of what it means to be a workplace designer if you take the role seriously. Which means that every well-designed project aligns with a larger strategy and helps to move it forward.

Form follows strategy. That's the essence of the workplace revolution from my perspective.

AVERAGE COMBINED WEEKLY HOURS
WORKED BY MARRIED COUPLES

# *flexible time*

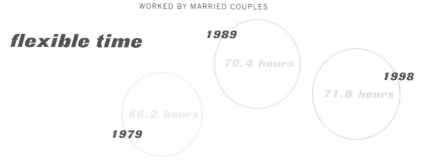

**1989**

*70.4 hours*

**1998**

*71.8 hours*

*66.2 hours*

**1979**

SHARE OF FULL-TIME WORKERS
WITH FLEXIBLE SCHEDULES

| | |
|---|---|
| *university teachers* | **65%** |
| *natural scientists* | **65%** |
| *mathematicians, computer scientists* | **59%** |
| *executives, managers* | **42%** |
| *household workers* | **41%** |
| *technicians* | **31%** |
| *salespeople* | **30%** |
| *administrators* | **23%** |
| *food service workers* | **22%** |
| *mechanics* | **18%** |
| *construction workers* | **18%** |
| *health service workers* | **18%** |
| *equipment cleaners* | **14%** |
| *machine operators* | **10%** |

M. Arthur Gensler Jr., FAIA, FIIDA, RIBA, is chairman and CEO
of Gensler, America's largest architecture and design firm, and a
leading specialist in workplace strategy and design.

1.  Karen Stephenson, "Don't Merge Without a Map" in *Dialogue*
    (Gensler Client Newsletter) no. 1 (1999).

FULL-TIME EMPLOYEES WORKING
FLEXIBLE SCHEDULES

*12.4%*

**1985**

*15.1%*

**1991**

*27.6%*

**1997**

Source: Bureau of Labor Statistics

**Filing department of the Metropolitan Life Insurance Company;** 1890s; New York, New York; Courtesy Museum of the City of New York, Byron Collection (93.1.1.6910)

The filing section at Metropolitan Life was primarily staffed by women. In order to insure a respectable office environment for its female employees, the company segregated men from women and enforced strict dress codes.

**Postcard, Equitable Building;** 1915; New York, New York; Architect: E.R. Graham

American sociologist C. Wright Mills called the office building an "enormous file" for the storage of paper—a description that certainly fit the Equitable Building. When this speculative real-estate project was completed in 1915, it was the world's largest office building, with 1.2 million square feet of rental space. The building's H-shaped plan increased its perimeter wall and window surface, which brought natural light into every office. Efficient elevators further allowed the developer to maximize the lot's financial potential.

# *introduction*

**Donald Albrecht and Chrysanthe B. Broikos**

The office building has represented the face of American business to the world throughout the twentieth century. Who can picture New York City without conjuring up the Empire State Building and the twin towers of the World Trade Center? Or San Francisco without invoking the Transamerica Tower? Or Chicago without the black silhouettes of the Sears Tower and John Hancock Center? These iconic structures—suggestive of the nation's economic and technological prowess—have made indelible impressions on the modern imagination. Yet behind these famous facades is another compelling story of modern development: the evolution of the American office.

The office is a microcosm of American social transformation and a yardstick of cultural progress. National dialogs between freedom and control, the individual and the crowd, private agendas and public concerns, personal mobility and communal connection are played out in the office. The shifting interaction between building design, technology, finance, and employees has yielded a dynamic environment whose significance extends beyond its physical boundaries. The office has figured in American life as architecture, but it has also been on the job as an incubator of radical change.

Although the office has had an enduring role in this country's history, it wasn't until after 1900 that the modern office developed as we know it today—an exemplar of the science of business management, information systems, and construction technologies. Modernizing forces transforming post–Civil War America reached the nerve center of capitalism, the office, in the early decades of the twentieth century. As the economy's emphasis shifted from farm to factory and office, legions of employees joined the ranks of white-collar workers, and women entered the workplace in full force. Manuals codified office culture and procedures. New types of buildings were developed to

**1919**

53% services

47% goods

*goods to services*

**1998**  20% goods

80% services

accommodate these changes, and the office itself emerged as a showcase of innovations in design and technology.

The coming of age of the modern office reflected contemporaneous trends in business development. After the Civil War, the rise of "the company," a term derived from military parlance, necessitated a new level of bureaucracy—"middle" management. Employees were hired to implement marketing strategies, coordinate long-distance distribution networks, track sales performance, and perform myriad other tasks. They were assisted by salespeople and office clerks, who processed orders and facilitated correspondence. The paper chase had begun. In 1860, for example, the census indicated that about 750,000 persons were engaged in "professional service" and other managerial and "commercial" positions. Thirty years later, the 1890 census showed that the number had risen to 2,160,000, while in 1910 it more than doubled

again to 4,420,000. (The 1890 census also was the first major use of Herman Hollerith's tabulating punch cards that were the forerunners of the computer, inaugurating a tradition of government-endorsed technological innovations later adopted by business.) As social historian Thomas J. Schlereth noted, members of this new urban managerial class were active participants in the era's revolutionary changes in politics, leisure, education, and consumer culture.[1] In 1919, social critic Upton Sinclair coined the term "white collar" to describe this new stratum of capitalist worker, signifying a seismic shift in the American labor force.[2]

Women represented a major component of this new class. Although paid less than men, many women found that office work offered better pay and more freedom than factory jobs or domestic service. Between 1900 and 1920, the percentage of women in the labor force who were clerical workers zoomed from 2 to 12 percent.[3]

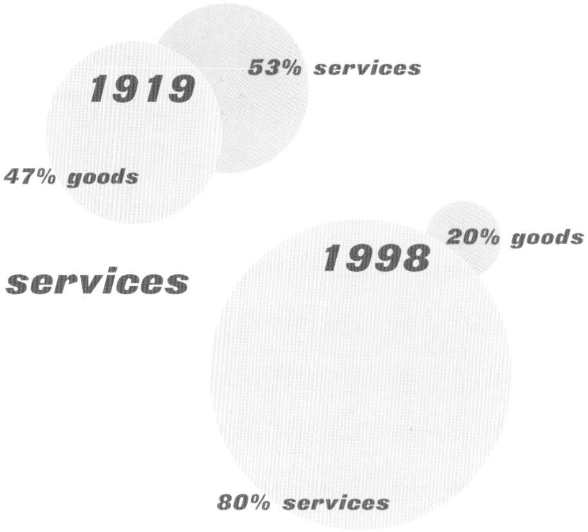

The economy's shift from goods to services has propelled the rise of the managerial class and the need for offices where they work. Source: U.S. Bureau of the Census, *Statistical Abstract of the United States: 1998*

**Tonya Scherba, software product manager at Evolve, Inc.** 2000; San Francisco, California; Photographer: Jeff Riedel © for the *New York Times*

Although some contemporary offices emphasize mobility and flexibility, most of the approximately 130 million Americans who make up the country's civilian work force are still bound to more traditional offices.

**Employees of the F.G. Day Compiling Company,** no date; Glenwood, Iowa; Courtesy Wittemann Collection, Prints and Photographs Division, Library of Congress

Business owners furnished and decorated the country's first offices in a domestic style, as seen in this photograph, probably from the Victorian era.

# *home and office*

the commute

**Advertisement, Guru.com,** 2000; Courtesy Guru.com and DDB Worldwide Communications Group

Consultants, independent contractors, or "free agents" often work at home where the coffee table doubles as a desk.

20
15
10
5
0

'90  '92  '93  '95  '97  '99

EMPLOYEES AND INDEPENDENT CONTRACTORS WORKING AT HOME AT LEAST ONE DAY A MONTH, IN MILLIONS

COMPANIES WITH WORK-AT-HOME OPTION

25
20
15
10
5
0

'93  '94  '95  '96  '97  '98

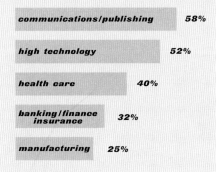

COMPANIES OFFERING TELECOMMUTING BY INDUSTRY IN 1997

| | |
|---|---|
| communications/publishing | 58% |
| high technology | 52% |
| health care | 40% |
| banking/finance insurance | 32% |
| manufacturing | 25% |

Sources: Cyber Dialogue, Joanne H. Pratt Associates, Hewitt Associates and Watson Wyatt Worldwide

A predominantly female workforce informed Frank Lloyd Wright's design for the unprecedented Larkin Administration Building in Buffalo, New York (1906). Conceived as the headquarters for the soap company's mail-order business, Larkin was the first office building to integrate innovations in architecture with progressive management philosophy, mechanical systems, spatial distribution, and furniture. Partly to attract the best workers (mostly women) and partly for public relations, Wright designed a clean, light-filled world completely separate from the gritty industrial environment around it. This monument to the progressive-era ideal of uplifting work, designed with the most advanced communications and distribution systems, also provided opportunities for employees' self-improvement: a YWCA, library, and music lounge.

Wright's Larkin Building established the office building as a testing ground for technological and design innovation. Throughout the twentieth century, elevators, steel-frame structural systems, fluorescent lighting, and metal and glass curtain walls were all eagerly embraced by both the design and business communities as ways to improve efficiency and productivity as well as profits. After World War II, air conditioning allowed people to work year round, day and night, virtually anywhere in the United States, forever changing the cyclical nature of commerce.

Business was also quick to adopt new office technologies, from typewriters to Dictaphones, fax machines to email, in its efforts to increase the speed, volume, and range of communications. As technologies changed, office design changed with them. Flexibility became the watchword of contemporary office design; modular wall, floor, and ceiling systems as well as workstations were developed to accommodate the constantly shifting dynamics of organizational structures and technical systems. Facilitating change has also driven design as

**Advertisement, Otis Elevator Company;** *Fortune*, September 1952

Otis introduced its attendant-free, "autotronic" elevator in 1950, just in time for the post-war building boom. Building managers and developers quickly adopted this new labor-and-cost-saving refinement of the traditional elevator.

**Advertisement, Benjamin Electric Manufacturing Company;** *Fortune*, September 1955

Targeted to executives, this ad noted that "it is not unusual for a new lighting system to pay for itself within 9 months in greater work output per employee and all-around efficiency." In the 1950s, as today, manufacturers and advertisers sought to quantify productivity gains in an attempt to relate design to the bottom line.

**Advertisement, Fenestra Electrifloor;** *Fortune,* March 1956

Electrifloor made it possible to move or add electrical outlets, telephones, intercoms, and other office machines by drilling through the floor. Easy access to power and communication lines was a major concern of the postwar office.

Drill for electricity...anywhere  ...with **ELECTRIFLOOR**

the structural floor system with unlimited electrical availability built right in

*Fenestra* | **ELECTRIFLOOR**

---

most office space has been speculatively built for unknown tenants with unknown needs.

Even some of the smallest innovations had tremendous impact on office life. The Modern Efficiency Desk, developed in 1915 for the Equitable Assurance Company's new Manhattan headquarters, was pivotal in the emergence of modern office culture. Little more than a table with shallow drawers, this new desk banished the privacy previously afforded by rolltop desks and the cabinetlike Wooton desk. Company managers preferred the new desk because it allowed them to easily survey workers and their work. The desk was also praised because it forced workers to keep office files and correspondence moving rather than hidden in the Wooton's myriad pigeonholes.

Aligned in orderly rows, the Modern Efficiency Desk symbolized the era's obsession with factory-like standardization and rational science. This was the period of Frederick Winslow Taylor's treatise on

scientific management and Ford Motor Company's development of the assembly line based on Taylor's studies. Time-and-motion studies shifted their focus from the factory to the office. Throughout the 1910s, Frank and Lillian Gilbreth, later memorialized in the best-selling novel *Cheaper by the Dozen,* applied assembly-line techniques to business, proposing ways to maximize the efficiency of office procedures from typing to rubber stamping.

While mass-production developments improved office productivity, they also unleashed a backlash of debate about standardization versus individuality. The boredom of the routinized workday, regulated by time clocks, was poignantly depicted in novels such as Sinclair Lewis's *The Job* (1917), the prototype for tales of office "working girls," and films like King Vidor's *The Crowd* (1928), which chronicled one man's internal struggle between his ambitious dreams and the crushing reality of quasi-military office life.

"No; the office is one thing, and private life is another. When I go into the office, I leave the Castle behind me, and when I come into the Castle, I leave the office behind me. If it's not in any way disagreeable to you, you'll oblige me by doing the same. I don't wish it professionally spoken about."

Charles Dickens, *Great Expectations*, 1860

**Advertisement, E.F. Hauserman Company;** *Fortune,* November 1956

Hauserman's baked-enamel office walls, offered in simulated wood or lively colors, were easy to maintain and reconfigure as business needs changed.

**Oxygen Media office,** 2000; New York, New York; Architect: Fernau & Hartman Architects; Photographer: Jason Schmidt © for the *New York Times*

In this rapidly expanding office, chairs and zipper desks are on wheels. Adaptability is prized in offices where work teams are shifted on a project-by-project basis.

**Order entry department at Sears, Roebuck and Company,** c. 1913; Chicago, Illinois; Courtesy Sears, Roebuck and National Museum of American History

Sears Roebuck's mail orders were processed at the company's catalog distribution center. Hundreds of women processed order forms in a huge space that looked more like a factory than an office.

**J. Louise O'Connor at her "decorated desk,"** 1916; United Shoe Machinery Company; Beverly, Massachusetts; Courtesy United Shoe Machinery Company Collection, Archives Center, National Museum of American History

Miss O'Connor's desk was decorated on the occasion of her wedding engagement (note the prominent placement of her left hand). Decorating the desks of men and women was a common office practice in the early decades of the twentieth century.

The office's image as a corporate barrack solidified after World War II. The war's successful military organization was mirrored in postwar America's management model of rigid hierarchies. Khaki-clad soldiers easily morphed into gray-flanneled businessmen. Complex emblems of their era, they were portrayed in various guises, from predictable drones in Robert Frank's 1955 *Fortune* magazine photo essay, *The Congressional,* to essential corporate tools in William H. Whyte's 1956 classic book, *The Organization Man,* and darkly comic cads in Billy Wilder's 1960 film, *The Apartment.*

. Although the dreary culture of Wilder's movie plagues American offices today—witness the popularity of Scott Adams's cubicle-bound cartoon hero, Dilbert®—a countermovement toward real flexibility in the workplace was emerging by the 1960s. During that decade, the development of such fields as human relations and environmental psychology helped to recast the office as a nurturing environment. New informal office layouts came to be called office landscapes or *"bürolandschaft,"* a term favored by the German Quickborner Consulting Group who revolutionized business design and initiated today's open office and flexible furniture systems.

Changes in the way America does business continue to transform the contemporary office. In the 1990s, the rise of the Internet, laptop computers, and telecommuting seemed to signal the demise of the conventional American office environment. Some of the country's leading management consulting firms and advertising agencies replaced offices and cubicles with mobile pedestals and telecommunications networks allowing employees to plug in and work virtually anywhere, anytime. As technology allowed decentralization of the workforce, corporate headquarters seemed headed for obsolescence.

Surprisingly, the recent growth of e-commerce has spurred a return to the office building—not the

**Poster, The Man in the Gray Flannel Suit,** 1956;
Courtesy Twentieth Century Fox Film Corporation.

Both the novel and film version of *The Man in the Gray Flannel Suit* helped shape a public portrait of corporate conformity in the 1950s.

conventional corporate glass and steel skyscraper, but nevertheless a centralized place where people gather, exchange ideas, and work. Contemporary idea-driven businesses have found that their success depends on collaboration between employees and clients and that their work environment needs to foster that interaction. Such businesses are creating homelike work environments where people can relax, share ideas, and be creative. The new corporate work places of the dot-com economy have kindergarten-like "romp spaces," coffee bars, gyms, day-care centers, pool tables, and dartboards. Spaces are provided for collaboration as well as private creative thought. Walled cubicles have been replaced by dynamic modular workstations on wheels that can be configured both as shared and as private areas. Innovative furnishings update the multitiered enclosures of vintage Wooton and roll-top desks. Managers are back in offices, but the offices are in the middle of work areas so they

mingle with employees throughout the day. The executive dining room and washroom are relics of the past. Instead, there are shared coffee bars and kitchens to minimize hierarchy and encourage company-wide interactions.

The appeal of the communal office environment has been reinforced by popular culture. Television programs such as *The Mary Tyler Moore Show* (1970–77), *LA Law* (1986–92), and *Ally McBeal* (1997– ) have charted the domesticated business realms where coworkers are surrogate families. Office life on *Murphy Brown* (1988–98), for example, unfolded in the show's shared newsroom-cum-kitchen. The recent introduction of a unisex bathroom in Ally McBeal's law firm moves the nation a step closer to understanding and accepting the contemporary office as a home away from home.

Exactly where one's office is has become less important in an age of email, cell phones, faxes, and teleconferencing. Whether these technologies

***The Crowd***, 1928; Courtesy
Metro-Goldwyn-Mayer Inc.
All rights reserved.

King Vidor's silent film classic
portrays the individual as a cog
in the machinery of corporate
efficiency and profitability.

## stocks and collars

The growth of American
business can be portrayed
through various barometers,
from the Dow Jones Industrial
Average (in red) to the number
of white-collar workers
(in thousands). "White collar"
means professional, technical,
managerial, and clerical workers.
Sources: © StockCharts.com
(All rights reserved) and U.S.
Bureau of the Census

"Look, no clutter on top or in drawers!"

SHAW-WALKER

will feel "real" enough for people to completely forgo face-to-face contact has yet to be determined. People will increasingly work at home, on airplanes, in restaurants—anywhere that new technologies reach. However, it seems likely that people will need human contact and the social cohesion of the office's physical space to be productive. More than any other single factor, this need suggests that the office, continuing to change into forms we can't yet imagine, is here to stay.

This publication, like the exhibition it accompanies, seeks to explore the dual role of the office as architectural and social space. In "Form Follows Fad: The Troubled Love Affair of Architectural Style and Management Ideal," James S. Russell looks at how America has been particularly receptive to new models of business philosophy, which has led to both extraordinary economic success and fad-driven failure, and he contrasts recent American and European designs. Stanley Abercrombie, in "Office Supplies: Evolving Furniture for the Evolving Workplace," traces the history of the workstation from Chippendale to George Nelson, Knoll, and beyond. Phil Patton's "Technology in the Office: Individual Power and Collective Standards" studies office technologies that have shaped the creation and flow of information both within the office and to the outside world. Finally, "Office Intrigues: The Interior Life of Corporate Culture," by Thomas Hine, examines how office interiors not only reflect corporate cultures but also project corporate identities to clients and the public. These articles are accompanied by four photographic essays of historic images as well as a newly commissioned essay by Steven Brooke, "New American Boomtown," on the Dulles High-Tech Corridor. Together, they demonstrate that the office remains an American obsession that is perennially celebrated, mocked, analyzed, and debated.

1. Thomas J. Schlereth, *Victorian America: Transformations in Everyday Life, 1876–1915* (New York: HarperPerennial, 1992), 29.

2. "It is a fact with which every union working man is familiar," Sinclair wrote, "that his most bitter despisers are the petty underlings of the business world, the poor office-clerks . . . who, because they are allowed to wear a white collar. . . , regard themselves as members of the capitalist class." Upton Sinclair, *Brass Check: A Study of American Journalism* (Pasadena, Calif.: the author, 1919), 78.

3. Alice Kessler-Harris, *Out of Work: A History of Wage-Earning Women in the United States* (New York: Oxford University Press, 1982), 148.

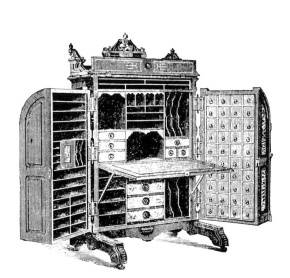

**Advertising graphic, Wooton Patent Cabinet Office Secretary manufactured by the Wooton Desk Company, Indianapolis, Indiana,** c. 1880; Courtesy Richard and Eileen Dubrow Antiques, Whitestone, New York

Advertised as "the desk of the age," the Wooton Secretary was first manufactured in 1874. A single key unlocked the cabinet's two wings, revealing pigeonholes, drawers, and a writing surface. When closed, the desk featured a letter slot for messages.

**Eddy workstation prototype,** 1997; Designer: Haworth Ideation Team; Courtesy Haworth

This cockpit-shaped workstation revives features of the Wooton desk, making office papers easy to reach and providing some sense of personal enclosure. Four concept models entitled Wake, Drift, Flo, and Eddy tested ideas and eventually led to the company's contemporary Crossings Office System.

# high-modern moment

**United Nations Secretariat Tower,** 1952; New York, New York; Architect: Wallace K. Harrison and Max Abramovitz, Le Corbusier (main idea) Photographer: Ezra Stoller © Esto

With the completion of the Secretariat, the United Nations's office tower, simple forms and metal-and-glass exterior walls came to symbolize a new international style of architecture. The facades' punch-card-like precision aligned this style with progressive American business and technology, helping to popularize this form of modern architecture throughout the postwar world.

If office buildings represent the face of American business, these classic images comprise a portrait gallery of mid-twentieth-century corporate culture. Such masterpieces as Lever House and John Deere's headquarters are the high-water mark of modernist office design, which was launched in the United States by the Philadelphia Savings Fund Society Building in 1932. After World War II, the gridded facade of the steel-and-glass office building, in the form of urban towers as well as suburban campuses, became the well-known emblem of a world based on international business and finance. "Form Follows Fad" puts this brilliant era in the context of a century of American office design, as high-style architecture, business, and culture joined forces in the 1950s and 1960s.
—D.A., C.B.B.

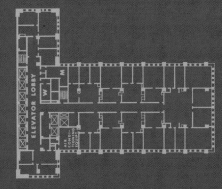

## *philadelphia savings fund society building*

1932; Philadelphia, Pennsylvania; Architect: Howe & Lescaze; Courtesy Hagley Museum and Library

# lever house

1952; New York, New York; Architect: Skidmore, Owings & Merrill
Photographer: Ezra Stoller © Esto

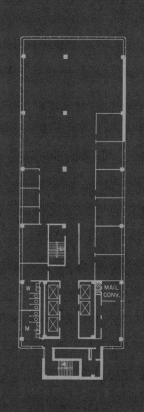

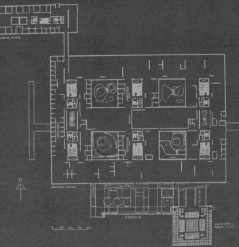

### *connecticut general headquarters*

1957; Bloomfield, Connecticut; Architect: Skidmore, Owings & Merrill; Interior designer: Knoll International with SOM;
Photographer: © Peter Mauss/Esto; (Connecticut General Life Insurance is now part of CIGNA)

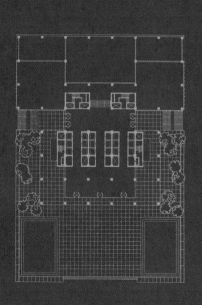
# *seagram building*

1958; New York, New York; Architect: Ludwig Mies van der Rohe
and Philip Johnson; Photographer: Ezra Stoller © Esto

# inland steel
# headquarters

1958; Chicago, Illinois; Architect: Skidmore, Owings & Merrill
Photographer: Bill Engdahl for Hedrich-Blessing; Courtesy
Chicago Historical Society

# *union carbide building*

1960; New York, New York; Architect: Skidmore, Owings & Merrill
Photographer: Ezra Stoller © Esto

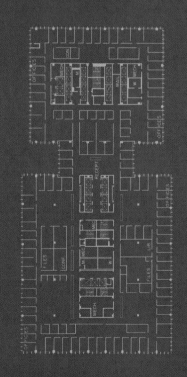

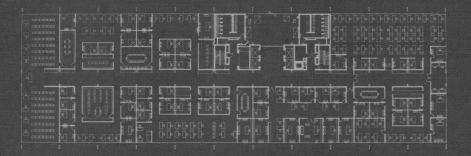

### *john deere headquarters*

1964; Moline, Illinois; Architect: Eero Saarinen and Associates; Photographer: Ezra Stoller © Esto;
Plan courtesy Kevin Roche John Dinkeloo and Associates

# *ford foundation headquarters*

1967; New York, New York; Architect: Kevin Roche John Dinkeloo and Associates; Landscape architect: Dan Kiley; Photographer: Ezra Stoller © Esto

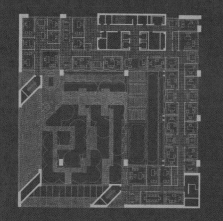

44

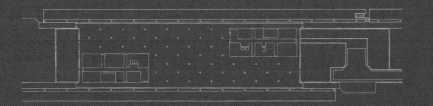

## weyerhauser headquarters

1971; Tacoma, Washington; Architect: Skidmore, Owings & Merrill; Interior designer: Knoll International with SOM;
Photographer: Ezra Stoller © Esto

**Atrium of the Larkin
Administration Building,** 1906;
Buffalo, New York;
Architect: Frank Lloyd Wright;
Courtesy Buffalo and Erie
County Historical Society

# form follows fad

## the troubled love affair of architectural style and management ideal

James S. Russell

Architects see themselves as pragmatic artists. Among themselves, architects talk about transforming the mundane necessities of factory life or office work to a higher cultural plane. To business clients, architects describe their skills in terms of problems they can solve and present their art as a powerful means to enhance business efficiency. But architecture advances in the hands of those driven by a personal aesthetic, if not a psychological agenda. The business client quickly recognizes this and often recoils. Business is never wholly comfortable making common cause with an endeavor that is not wholly devoted to its own agenda.

This is why architecture and business, over the decades of the twentieth century, have had much in common with the partners in a tempestuous love affair. American business has only intermittently succumbed to architecture's fascinations. After a dizzying courtship, business leaders often conclude that architecture, like a beautiful mistress,

too often consumes the bottom line rather than adding to it.

Architecture and engineering coalesced into professions defined by degrees and practice standards only at end of the nineteenth century. The professionalization of design coincided with management challenges posed by enormous growth in scale of turn-of-the-century industrial enterprise: Artisanal shops and steam-driven riverside mills employing from a dozen to a few hundred workers gave way to vast coal-fired factory complexes employing thousands. This enormous growth was accompanied by equally enormous dislocation: Work moved out of the home to vast canal- and railway-laced tracts at the edge of cities; the economy oscillated between fabulous growth and heart-stopping collapse; millions of immigrants pouring onto American shores appeared to challenge the social order. America consolidated its place as the leading industrial power against a background of relatively high labor costs and waves of worker unrest, symbolized most alarmingly (to business owners) in the incipient labor movement.

Proclaiming that "human happiness was a business asset," the industrial betterment movement seemed to offer an alternative to both unionization and eternal labor strife. The hands of workers would fly, the argument went, if they were well fed and housed and if they felt their success was intertwined with that of the company. Shaping the morality of the untutored worker or the immigrant new to America put a nurturing face on raw capitalism. John H. Patterson forged the success of the National Cash Register Company in Dayton, Ohio, through the "practical religion" of industrial betterment.[1]

Progressive companies one hundred years ago offered amenities readily recognized by the stock option-dazzled worker of today—not just lunchrooms, bathhouses, hospital clinics, and safety training but also recreational facilities, thrift clubs, benefit funds, and profit-sharing plans. The Larkin Company of Buffalo, New York, was the emblematic industrial betterment enterprise. It took an almost familial approach to staff, who were treated to picnics and weekly concerts and offered educational incentives and profit-sharing. In hiring Frank Lloyd Wright to design a new administration building, the company found an architect who possessed a messianic, Emersonian evangelism all his own. Wright proved the perfect person to put the Larkin ideal of moral uplift into place; in the process, he created one of the most conceptually and technically rich commercial buildings of the twentieth century.

When Wright was hired, in 1902, the Larkin Company produced a variety of soaps, perfumes, powders, and other household products in a two-million-square-foot complex at the industrial edge of Buffalo. Selling by mail order, Larkin helped lead America into the consumer era by offering premiums (which it made or purchased) to induce customers to place larger orders.[2]

In an economy overwhelmingly dedicated to manufacturing, Larkin presaged the shift to white-collar work. Wright was hired to build a structure to house the ever-expanding clerical staff that the mail-order and premium business required. The phenomenal growth sprang in part from a new, highly efficient account-tracking system developed by the company's secretary, Darwin D. Martin, who became one of Wright's most important clients.

Larkin executives recognized that the clerical staff, overwhelmingly women, needed a clean, well-lighted place to work—a feat not easily accomplished amid Buffalo's smoke-wrapped railroad sidings. Wright created a beautiful light-filled interior and, he is justly celebrated in history for the inventive way he filtered the fetid air. But he also made a highly efficient machine of work, using emerging technology to handle the thousands of items of correspondence that poured in daily. From a lower-level receiving area, mail was moved to the upper levels, then processed downward. Wright installed cabinets in alcoves below high windows for Martin's system of card filing. Company correspondents dictated responses to inquiries into gramophones, which were taken by messengers to a typing pool, then checked and mailed.[3]

The building also provided numerous self-improvement opportunities for the Larkin "family": a library, lounge, YWCA, and classroom. The solid piers of the central light court gave way, as they soared upward, to elaborate decorations, hanging plants, and the sun's rays picking out gold-leafed inspirational inscriptions. The celestial reference was none too subtle. In the public areas, wrote historian Jack Quinan, "sculptures and inscriptions

**Built-in filing cabinets in the Larkin Building,** 1906; Buffalo, New York; Architect: Frank Lloyd Wright; Courtesy Buffalo and Erie County Historical Society

**Larkin Building,** 1906;
Courtesy The Frank Lloyd
Wright Archives, Scottsdale,
Arizona

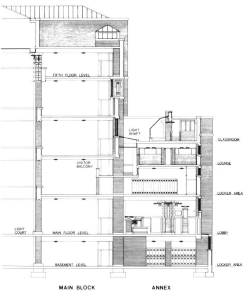

**Section of the Larkin Building;**
Delineator: James Cahill;
Courtesy Jack Quinan

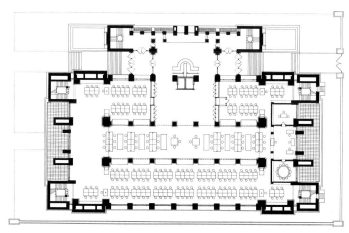

**Ground floor plan of the
Larkin Building;** Redrawn by
Joseph Bruno, Charles Rhyu,
Toby O'Rorke, Dragan Mrdja,
and Brian Messina; Courtesy
the Museum of Modern Art,
New York

**Typing department at the National Cash Register Company,** c. 1890; Dayton, Ohio; Courtesy NCR Archive at the Montgomery County Historical Society

**Wall inscriptions in the atrium of the Larkin Building,** 1906; Courtesy Buffalo and Erie County Historical Society

directed the employees away from the common notion of work as mindless drudgery and toward the belief that work well done is inherently edifying."[4] The most prominent inscription reads, "Ask and it shall be given you. Seek and ye shall find. Knock and it shall be opened unto you." This evangelical quality is as much Wright as it is Larkin. Throughout his life, Wright studded his talks and writing with such comments on poetry, truth, beauty, and ideals.

Wright's administration building played a key part in the Larkin Company's growth and success until the mid-1920s, when the departure of the men key to its success led to a slow decline. Larkin tried to rejuvenate itself by establishing retail outlets (including one in the famous atrium), but the company stumbled into dissolution by 1943. The building, abandoned, was demolished in 1950 in spite of a national outcry—it is, arguably, the greatest of Wright's lost buildings.

The workplace architecture of moral uplift exemplified by the Larkin Building saw its grandest, skyscraping apogee in the soaring neo-Gothic terracotta shaft of New York's 1913 Woolworth Building. Such idealism, however, did not survive the horror of World War I nor the giddy consumer culture of the 1920s.

### "a normal American madness"

Another management ideal arose parallel to industrial betterment. It, too, challenged architects in the design of the workplace. The systemizers, according to progressive-era historian Samuel Haber, struggled to wean American industry from its reliance on improvisation and individual initiative and fought for rationalism in industrial methods and the centralization of authority, hierarchy, and discipline akin to that of a military organization.[5]

Frederick Winslow Taylor, the father of scientific management, was the most famous systemizer and ranks among the oddest figures in business history—no small feat in an era bursting with eccentrics. Born in 1856 into genteel Quaker Philadelphia affluence, he early demonstrated that he was no ordinary child. He exasperated his playmates, for example, by insisting on measuring a court for a game of rounders in exact feet and inches.[6] And he made lists of girls expected to attend a school dance, categorizing them as either attractive or unattractive, so that he could efficiently make use of time others regarded as carefree.

Though his keen intelligence, along with his father's insistence, predestined him to Harvard and a career in law, Taylor left Phillips Exeter Academy just prior to completing his studies, an apparent victim of debilitating headaches and failing eyesight. After a few months' recuperation, he renounced the path his father had set for him and, instead, joined the Enterprise Hydraulic Works in Philadelphia as an apprentice pattern maker and machinist. He moved on to the city's Midvale Steel Company where he worked his way up the ladder becoming Midvale's chief engineer. Taylor began to apply his analytical mind and mania for measurement to hone the efficiency of production by recording and analyzing tasks, measuring how long they took, and identifying methods that would save time and motion.

As Taylor took his proposals to other companies, he was surprised to find resistance. In his methods to engineer industrial processes, workers saw the potential for more work by fewer hands for less money. Taylor's imperious manner likewise failed to endear him to management, which saw a threat to comforting old ways. He was even opposed by his employers, the bosses who would presumably benefit. They never invested enough money nor gave his methods enough time to work, he bitterly complained. His ideas began to catch fire, however, as disciples with greater diplomatic skill took over the hands-on tasks, leaving Taylor to consulting and writing. His most famous work was the 1911 book, *The Principles of Scientific Management.*[7]

Louis Brandeis, who later became an influential Supreme Court justice, inadvertently made Taylor famous by using Taylorite principles to argue the Eastern Rate Case of 1910–11. While the case nominally concerned the arcane question of rail freight rates, it became a lightning rod for a nation made anxious by inflation. Brandeis, who represented interests who would have to pay more if rates were increased, made a stirring case suggesting that the railroads obviously didn't need more money because they were not using modern efficiency techniques.

Suddenly, efficiency became the new panacea for the price problem. This "normal American madness," as it was famously dubbed, "hit like a flash flood," according to historian Haber, "at first covering almost the entire landscape, but soon collecting in various places to be absorbed slowly and to enrich the immediate surroundings. . . . Efficiency appeared as a refurbishment of the commonplace exhortations to virtue and duty, as a means for the transference of personal morality to society, and as a means for the control of society without specific reference to morality."[8]

Taylor and his Taylorites were relentlessly attacked over ensuing years, especially by labor activists who decried his belief in the necessity of people "in an organization to become one of a train of gear wheels."[9] But Taylor's focus on analytical methods rankled America for another reason: It appeared to subsume American individual intuition and enterprise to the mechanistic methods of science.

Haber remarked on how "Taylor's frenzy for order was the counterpart of the disorder within him." Sudhir Kakar, who wrote a psychobiography of Taylor, found a man who was perpetually "propitiating vindictive and wrathful gods" within himself.[10]

Whatever those gods may have been, Taylor found himself unable to escape them. He compulsively measured, analyzed, and sought improvements in just about everything he encountered. He even invented a golf putter to improve his game. Frederick Taylor died in 1915, his death signaled by his failure to arise at exactly his usual hour and wind his Swiss watch.

### engineering the workplace — and the nation

One of Taylor's fondest dreams was that scientific management would establish the primacy of engineers in business management. The profession seemed more embattled the more the nation took as its watchword the greatest value for the least money expended. While engineers' fondest desire was to extend the state of the art, business owners complained that their time and money were too valuable to underwrite reinvention of the wheel.

Herbert Croly, a journalist and critic who edited the *Architectural Record* in the early years of the twentieth century, found much the same pressures applied to architects. Haber summed up Croly's frequent writings for the magazine: "There was little instinctive love of art in America, Croly declared. The great mass of building in this country was directed by men who were simply trying to build for as little money as possible something which would sell or rent. Even those who seemed concerned with beauty had the most barbarous taste. Art, which in most countries grew almost unconsciously, in America had to be pursued consciously, if at all."[11]

Recognizing how difficult it was to raise the status of architecture, Croly came to believe, with Brandeis and critic Walter Lippman, that professionals deserved a special status whereby their disinterested wisdom and acuity could be applied to the problems of the country. The expertise of the well-trained professional elite would keep at bay both the worst instincts of business and the inchoate desires of the masses. Croly's famous and influential book, *The Promise of American Life,* was published in 1909. In it, he proposed that the nation be run by "exceptional men" rather than "the popular average."[12] Such an elite could reengineer the economy and the polity to improve the status of the wretched poor and mend the social chasms that yawned between uneducated foreigners and the middle class that felt threatened by them.

In short, the "efficiency experts" that were rationalizing business would be turned to the task to rationalizing government. The primacy of science and professionalism in public affairs obtained a nationwide advocate in the *New Republic* magazine, which debuted in 1914 with Croly as editor. Progressive reformer Thorstein Veblen took up the call after World War I, making common cause with followers of Taylor and suggesting a separate elevated role for engineers to control and foster "productive efficiency" in the nation as a whole. It was not to be. The movement quickly dissolved, with Veblen blaming engineers' "hired-man's loyalty to the established order."[13]

### workers at the mercy of their environment

No professional cadre ever officially ran the country, nor did such larger-than-life individuals as Taylor or Croly ever again propose a crucial, decision-making role for professionals in a capitalist society. Instead, the scale of enterprise grew ever larger, spurring research intended to define the degree to which the design of the environment could measurably affect productivity.

In 1924, the Hawthorne Works, a Western Electric Company telephone assembly plant in Chicago, was the site of what became a highly influential study, sponsored by the National Academy of Sciences.[14] Researchers increased and decreased workplace illumination and measured the effect of each level on productivity. They were dumbfounded by the lack of consistency in the results. As they raised lighting levels, productivity improved in some departments, but not in all. In one area, productivity not only improved but stayed at the higher level even when lighting levels were lowered. (Workers in that department were paid by the piece, so they already had considerable incentive to work quickly.) Researchers added and subtracted variables, attempting to isolate a productivity-illumination relationship, but still found no correlation of illumination to performance. Later researchers concluded that the recognition by workers that they were being studied had more effect on their productivity than the environmental changes did. This came to be called the Hawthorne Effect.

The Hawthorne Effect appeared to reveal that attitudes toward work and relationships with coworkers and supervisors were far more important than the quality of the physical environment. Though the assumed relationships between environmental factors and efficiency came to be regarded as too simplistic and mechanistic as posed by the studies, the word got out to the business community at large: The quality of the workplace was not especially important to workers.

### mechanization takes command

It took World War II, which ushered in many unanticipated changes in American life, to again alter the relationship between architects and business. Mechanical ventilation, air conditioning, and improved fluorescent lighting were innovations that mobilization for war turned into necessities. The mechanically serviced workplace came into its own as windows, skylights, and light monitors—traditional forms of lighting and ventilation—were sealed to meet wartime blackout requirements.

The war also had a dramatic decentralizing effect. Industrial districts and downtowns made tantalizing targets, so the military encouraged the location of strategic research and manufacturing facilities away from built-up urban areas and existing factory districts. Plenty of good locations had been created along the extensive highway network put in place as a Depression make-work effort. After the war, few suburban facilities returned to central cities.[15]

Even more important, organizations found that people worked efficiently in serried ranks of desks with few traditional amenities or architectural embellishments—at least under the pressures of wartime. A legendary example is the humble, wood-framed Building 20, hurriedly erected in 1943 as a temporary site for the development of radar at the Massachusetts Institute of Technology. Until recently it was still standing, having incubated not only wartime advances but also the science of linguistics, research in nuclear science, cosmic rays, dynamic analysis and control, acoustics, food technology, as well as numerous computer breakthroughs.[16] In the postwar era, business began to question whether architecture deserved a role in the workplace any more sophisticated than as a drafting service.

### "organizations seek the adaptable, interchangeable person"

The way the war changed architecture was not immediately apparent. Business architecture in the two decades after the end of the war entered a kind of golden age. Companies wanted to put a face on the increasing importance of advancing technology in business success and economic growth. This coincided with American architects' belated love affair with European modernism. Architects defined a new image for business by clipping lightweight metal-and-glass membranes to steel skeleton frames, displacing masonry and terra cotta. Pietro

Belluschi's Equitable Building in Portland, Oregon, led the way in 1948. Its flush skin was fabricated of war-surplus aluminum and its windows were glazed in an early version of sealed, insulated glass. It used a deep well to sink excess heat from the building.[17]

In the 1950s, Skidmore, Owings & Merrill alone designed such canonical office towers as Lever House (New York, 1952), Inland Steel (Chicago, 1958), and Union Carbide (now Chase Manhattan, New York, 1960). When businesses moved to the suburbs, they hired architects to build a more modern, progressive image of the corporation, offering views to lavishly designed leafy landscapes rather than the sooty exteriors of other buildings. Gordon Bunshaft of Skidmore, Owings & Merrill set a long, low, prismatic glass square on farmland in Bloomfield, Connecticut, for the Connecticut General Life Insurance Company (1957), punching out four courtyards landscaped as Japanese gardens. Nearby, he perched a 336- by 378-foot tray of horizontal space on branching riblike fingers springing from concrete trunks for the Emhart Manufacturing Company in 1963.

At the mammoth General Motors Technical Center in Warren, Michigan (1956), Eero Saarinen placed bulletlike air-handling nozzles in a metal ceiling grid otherwise made of luminous panels. The 1960s and 1970s witnessed an even more sophisticated integration of mechanical and electrical systems. Air conditioning became universal in the United States, leading to the sealed buildings that are still standard. While a variety of systems were developed to feed cooling, heating, and lighting from the ceiling, trenches cast into the floor routed the growing networks of electrical wiring and telephones upward into desks. Standard modules were applied to column spans, window-wall systems, lighting systems, office dividers, and furniture to make space utilization more efficient and workstations interchangeable. The workspaces of the late

**Lobby of the Research
Administration Building of the
General Motors Technical Center,**
1956; Warren, Michigan; Architect:
Eero Saarinen and Associates;
Photographer: Ezra Stoller © Esto

**Equitable Building,** 1948;
Portland, Oregon;
Architect: Pietro Belluschi;
Photographer: Ezra Stoller © Esto

**Emhart Manufacturing headquarters,**
1963; Shelton, Connecticut;
Architect: Skidmore, Owings & Merrill;
Photographer: Ezra Stoller © Esto

**Advertisement, Honeywell;**
*Fortune*, June 1959

Honeywell's "Selectographic
Supervisory DataCenter"
allowed a single operator to
monitor, adjust, and control the
air-conditioning system of an
entire building.

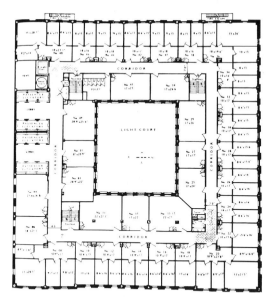

Plan, Strauss Building, 1924;
Chicago, Illinois; Architect:
Graham, Anderson, Probst and
White; Courtesy Carol Willis

## This Suite at $130 a Month

*in Chicago's Finest Office Building*

Advertisement, Strauss Building,
1923; Chicago, Illinois;
Courtesy Carol Willis

1960s were well lit, well ventilated, and insulated from noise to a degree unimaginable a decade and a half earlier.[18]

For all their design bravura and technological sophistication, buildings through the first two post-war decades expressed an almost unchanged management view of the workplace. Elaborate hierarchies emulated the military bureaucracies that had successfully prosecuted the war. "Organizations seek the adaptable, interchangeable person," William H. Whyte wrote in his seminal 1956 study, *The Organization Man*.[19] The gridded, rationalized, evenly serviced, and totally flexible nature of the architectural workspace perfectly reflected the war-era management zeitgeist.

What was missing from the postwar era was a role for architects beyond the elegant packaging of such anonymous, undifferentiated space. It seems ironic that the periods of greatest prosperity—and, consequently, of greatest construction—in the twentieth century coincided with a minimized role for architects.

The trend began in the 1920s. Though the era is famous for such exuberant structures as the neo-Gothic Chicago Tribune Building (1924) and the jazz-age glitter of the Chrysler Building (1930), architects devoted far more of their attention to proficiently turning out buildings that delivered the most rentable area per square foot built. They lamented the increasing complexity of the task and the greater numbers of experts whose concerns had to be accommodated. "The owner and his practical advisers must test and pass upon the plan and its functioning," wrote R.H. Shreve, a partner of Shreve, Lamb & Harmon, designers of the Empire State Building (1931). "Finance dictates the fenestration; rent rolls rule the 'parti.' The engineers, the builder, and the Building Department impose material limitations affecting color and texture, while the zoning law and the budget cast their shadows over form

and mass—ancient domains of my Lord Architect—now jointly occupied by him and his allies in the name of Cooperation."[20] While architects today might not frame the issue in such colorful prose, they readily recognize the sentiment.

The soaring shafts, Mayan ziggurats, zigzag decorations, and neo-Gothic finials that characterized the 1920s skyscrapers enclosed plans honed to minimize unrentable hallways. Windows were arranged not according to expressive whim but to allow emerging office-plan layout specialists to regularize the size of offices. Skyscraping machines for moneymaking, such as Chicago's Strauss Building (1924), became the defining structures of the twentieth-century American city.

In the high-growth era that followed World War II, the attention lavished on the palatial quarters erected for the postwar corporate elite disguised a much broader trend to dispense with all but the most minimal attention of the architect. The wartime experience had shattered the consensus that business needed architecture to put on a certain kind of appropriately civic face. As suburbs leapfrogged into the leafy hinterlands, commercial architecture became ever more standardized, with more and more parts selected from catalogs and subassembled in factories for quick erection on site. Croly's concern that "the great mass of building in this country was directed by men who were simply trying to build for as little money as possible" only became more evident as the second half of the century unfolded.

### the office as a landscape

Salvation for architects had to come from finding a new way to use facilities to add value to the bottom line. The 1960s promised a reexamination of the role of environment in nurturing better performance as the management era of human relations emerged along with the field of environmental psychology. Not since the Hawthorne studies had such attention been given to office design in relation to staff satisfaction and performance. Researchers began to analyze methods of communication among groups, the development of team solidarity, and the role of physical proximity in the functioning of teams and groups of teams. In Europe, social welfare policies led to calls for more equality among employees, less emphasis on status and authority, and a greater staff voice in management decision making.

None of these ideas found architectural expression until brothers Wolfgang and Eberhard Schnelle, who worked in their father's office furniture business, founded the Quickborner Consulting Group outside Hamburg, Germany. Offices should be laid out on the basis of close communication as well as efficient workflow, they claimed. Private offices and other badges of status should be eliminated in the service of easier teamwork and wider staff participation. Quickborner layouts were fluid, almost literally echoing the curving lines of diagrams drawn to reflect lines of communication. Such informal layouts came to be called *bürolandschaft* or office landscapes.[21]

One of the pioneering installations was for Osram, a Munich-based lighting manufacturer whose administration building was designed by Walter Henn in 1963. Planters demarcated winding passageways among hivelike functional groupings. Private offices were eliminated for all but senior staff to emphasize the value of communication over hierarchy.[22]

In the United States, the *bürolandschaft* concept attracted enormous attention. "After years of having nothing to discuss," wrote interior-design consultant John Pile, the design community "seized on landscaping as the most interesting and controversial development in sight." A widely publicized early American example was the 1967 installation designed by Hans J. Lorenzen for Du Pont's Freon Products Division in Wilmington, Delaware.[23] But the concept quickly attracted critics, who derided its lack of privacy, the noise and distractions endemic to the office's openness, and the lower status conveyed by the lack of a private office.

Americans, characteristically, reworked the curvilinear informality of the Quickborner system into something cheaper and more ordered. Open office environments were perfect for "systems furniture," highly flexible combinations of desks and dividing panels. Each workstation could be extensively customized by mounting shelves, cabinets, and accessories on the panels, and it could be as readily demounted and reconfigured. An early system, Herman Miller's Action Office II of 1968, was based on a five-foot hexagonal module.[24]

One aspect American business owners did not fail to notice was that open plan workstations took up much less space and were cheaper to build and easier to rearrange than conventional layouts. Open plan offices and systems furniture caught on in the 1970s but quickly evolved into the regimented ranks of cubicles familiar to white-collar workers today.

At the same time, businesses began to recognize that white-collar work was more than pushing paper—it was pushing ideas. Companies needed more flexible and interactive ways of conveying and working with knowledge. The Ford Foundation Building in New York wrapped offices around a soaring atrium space (Kevin Roche John Dinkeloo and Associates, 1967). The terrraced court at its base, an oasis of verdant tropical growth, was laced with paths and places to pause. It not only gave its staff views of this welcome patch of green at the center of the city, it glorified a stroll-in-the-park metaphor for engendering and sharing ideas. Architect Herman Herzberger built a multilevel city within a city in his Centraal Beheer offices for an insurance

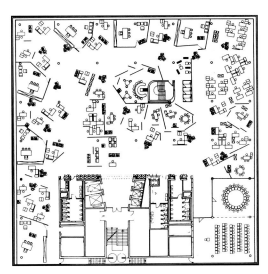

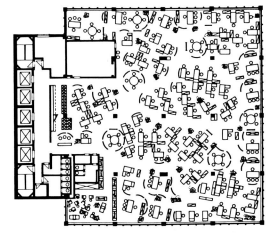

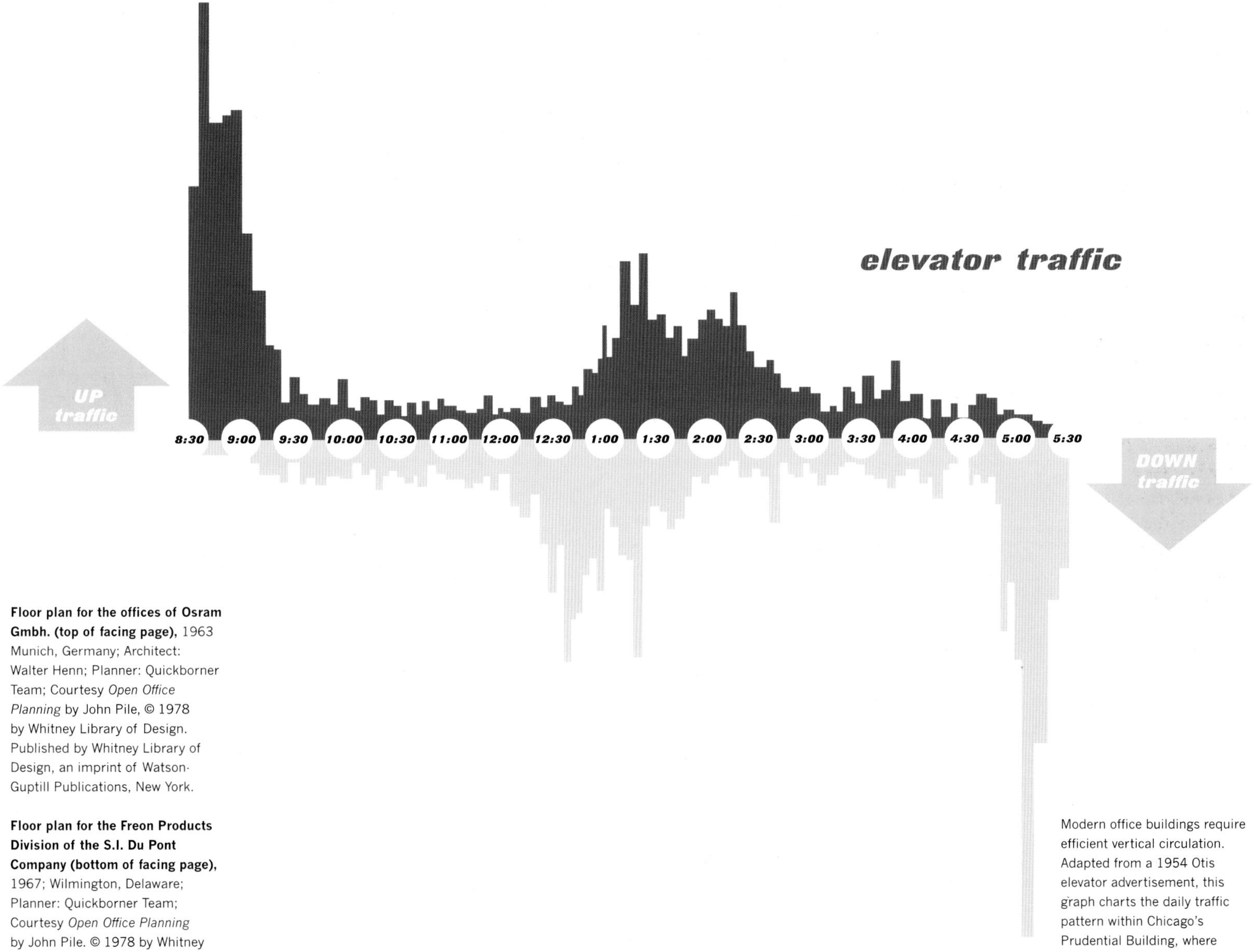

*elevator traffic*

UP traffic

DOWN traffic

8:30  9:00  9:30  10:00  10:30  11:00  12:00  12:30  1:00  1:30  2:00  2:30  3:00  3:30  4:00  4:30  5:00  5:30

**Floor plan for the offices of Osram Gmbh. (top of facing page),** 1963 Munich, Germany; Architect: Walter Henn; Planner: Quickborner Team; Courtesy *Open Office Planning* by John Pile, © 1978 by Whitney Library of Design. Published by Whitney Library of Design, an imprint of Watson-Guptill Publications, New York.

**Floor plan for the Freon Products Division of the S.I. Du Pont Company (bottom of facing page),** 1967; Wilmington, Delaware; Planner: Quickborner Team; Courtesy *Open Office Planning* by John Pile. © 1978 by Whitney Library of Design. Published by Whitney Library of Design, an imprint of Watson-Guptill Publications, New York.

Modern office buildings require efficient vertical circulation. Adapted from a 1954 Otis elevator advertisement, this graph charts the daily traffic pattern within Chicago's Prudential Building, where twenty-seven automatic elevators completed an estimated sixty thousand passenger rides every day.

company in Apeldoorn, Holland (1972). Networks of pods, each containing four spaces, branched off a series of towers. The internal pods looked out on toplit, casbahlike passageways. By introducing a village scale to the office, Herzberger hoped to encourage a humanistic entrepreneurialism among workers who could adapt spaces for personal needs or combine them for group work.[25]

In 1975, architect Norman Foster explored an emerging urban metaphor for work in the Willis Faber and Dumas building located in Ipswich, England. While much of the space was taken up by a gridded layout of open plan cubicles, Foster united the four-level complex with a waterfall of escalators that tumbled down to the lobby from a skylighted top-floor cafeteria, which itself opened onto a sodded rooftop eating area. These appealing social spaces emulated the casual encounters people might have walking down a city street. The idea was that, as they lingered around the escalators or lounged on the landscaped roof, staff would incubate better ways of doing things. In an intriguing twist of the industrial betterment idea, a swimming pool, glassed in at street level, became a kind of corporate shop window to cue passersby to the company's benevolence.[26]

### the building breathes

Such innovations were the exception, however. The fizzling of *bürolandschaft* in America was nothing like the backlash against it that occurred in Europe. The social-democratic politics that prevailed in Scandinavia, Germany, and Holland empowered workers' councils, who put the quality of the office environment on the bargaining table. Not only did workers' councils decry the distractions and lack of privacy innate to the open office, they hated the large, deep floors, where people had to sit as far as one hundred feet from the nearest window. Since the 1970s, the councils have made private or semi-private offices the norm for a high percentage of white-collar workers. Access to an operable window opening onto a view is now mandated in much of Northern Europe.

Thus began an enormous divergence between American and European office design practice. The need to give nearly every office a window inspired a great deal of architectural innovation in Europe. Deep, squarish plans got stretched into long, narrow slabs or starfish shapes. Such long wings, however, tended to isolate workers. In 1988, the SAS headquarters in Stockholm, designed by Niels Torp, arranged narrow, fingerlike office wings along a skylighted internal street. Lined with plant-draped lounges and coffee bars, the street became the focus of company life, a place where meetings could occur informally and where process-improving ideas might emerge over a cup of coffee.[27]

The push for a window and fresh air came out of an ecological sensibility and a suspicion of mechanically treated air that is deep seated in the culture of many Northern European countries. Dutch, Danish, and German workers are also much more likely to bike to work than Americans, so it was only natural for Europe to take the lead in pushing energy-conserving and environmentally sustainable building technologies through a combination of sponsored research, tax benefits, and prototype projects.

In 1994, a bright blue airframe-shaped tube of a building, poised on insectlike legs, came to completion: the Hôtel du Département des Bouches-du-Rhone, a government administration building for the Marseilles region of France. Its shape, a competition-winning design by the British-German architecture firm Alsop & Störmer, was sculpted to drive prevailing breezes through the building. A paddlelike device over the naturally ventilated atrium rotated to reflect light into the space on dim days and block it on bright ones.[28]

**Centraal Beheer Insurance Company,** 1972; Apeldoorn, Holland; Architect: Herman Herzberger; Photographer: © Richard Bryant; Courtesy Arcaid

**Atrium of the Willis Faber
and Dumas Building,** 1975;
Ipswich, England;
Architect: Foster and Partners;
Photographer: John Donat;
Courtesy Foster and Partners

**"Main Street" of the SAS
headquarters,** 1988;
Stockholm, Sweden;
Architect: Niels Torp AS;
Courtesy Niels Torp

**Hôtel du Département des
Bouches-du-Rhone,** 1994;
Marseilles, France;
Architect: Alsop & Störmer;
Courtesy Stratton & Reekie

**Commerzbank,** 1997; Frankfurt,
Germany; Architect: Foster and
Partners; Photographer:
© Ralph Richter/Architekturphoto

Foster and Partners completed an ambitious "eco-skyscraper" in Frankfurt for Commerzbank in 1997. The architects drew a triangular plan with bulging sides, then drilled a generous atrium out of the center of the full thirty-story height of the tower. To bring light and air into the atrium, Foster punched a series of "sky gardens" out of the sides of the building. It was a breathtaking advance on the communitarian office ideal that first took form in the Ford Foundation building.

It not only gave all the offices an outside window, it transformed the entire experience of working in a tall building. Most tower occupants have a sense of themselves as individuals because they look out over a skyline of strangers and competitors. There is little connection with colleagues who work on other floors. At Commerzbank, occupants of atrium-facing offices not only see the sky through the garden openings, they see colleagues at work on floors above and below. Individuals are palpably reminded that they are part of a larger organization. The gardens, shared by several floors, make readily accessed meeting places.[29]

### rise of the real-estate product

Something quite different happened in the United States beginning in the late 1970s. Businesses came to see the office building as a profit-making asset in its own right and began managing it for ultimate sale or sublease rather than for long-term value. Instead of erecting buildings that reflected community commitment, corporate values, or the needs of business process, companies began to shave away every eccentricity; this approach was dictated by a real-estate development mentality that focused entirely on delivering a completely generic product produced at lowest first cost. The floor plan shape and size of the American office building became rigidly proscribed nationwide. It grew increasingly difficult for architects to propose specific solutions to a client's unique needs or site. As such buildings were dumbed down to real-estate development product, innovation withered.

In quantity of commercial construction, the early 1980s had no equal, thanks to lax lending requirements and generous tax benefits. While renewed status consciousness brought back the private office, it was, like the 1920s and 1950s, an era in which architects and interior designers were offered few opportunities to create innovative expressions of business goals. "Prestige" projects were denoted by the elaborateness of materials applied to the lobby and the complexity of the building crown. Under their neo-Deco, neo-Flemish, even neo-Gothic skins, the buildings hardly differed.

### from garages to caves, clubs, and hives

The collapse of commercial building construction that occurred in the late 1980s coincided with an era of massive restructuring and downsizing in American business. Companies discovered "total quality" and learned the lessons American W. Edwards Deming had so successfully taught the Japanese. They went *In Search of Excellence* (the title of Tom Peters's and Robert H. Waterman's wildly successful management bible); they became "customer driven," according to the tenets of Richard C. Whitely, or "reengineered" their corporations, as advised by Michael Hammer and James Champy.[30]

As accounting firms branched out to offer a broad range of management consulting services, they were among the first to recognize the businesses that they were restructuring might benefit from new kinds of physical spaces. Management consultants created a new type of shared space for "road warriors"—home bases for consultants who spent most of their time on the premises of clients. A "concierge" set up the space, with files, computer hookup, and telephone, all arranged on a daily basis like a hotel room—hence the ugly term "hoteling."

Business began paying attention to a body of research on building design for emerging work methodologies by the likes of the Buffalo Organization for Social and Technological Innovation (BOSTI, led by Michael Brill), Franklin Becker (of Cornell University's International Workplace Studies Program), and Francis Duffy (of London-based DEGW, an architectural firm that specialized in a strategic approach to workplace design).[31] A variety of office environments emerged in the 1990s, each with a catchy name: free address and group address, just-in-time space, caves, commons, hives, and clubs. Most were intended to recognize flattened corporate hierarchies and encourage new kinds of teamwork that united a great number of traditionally separate disciplines such as manufacturing, engineering, and marketing.[32]

More important than the entirely unconventional appearance of the offices Jay Chiat built in New York and California for his Chiat/Day advertising agency was that he eliminated conventional workstations and offices. In offices designed by Gaetano Pesce and Frank Gehry (with Claes Oldenburg and Coosje van Bruggen, later altered by Lubowicki/Lanier Architects), he invited staff—equipped with portable phone and laptop computer—to become nomads, choosing a place to work based on what they needed to do that day. Depending on who you believe, Chiat sold the company a few years after these offices were completed because (a) he had given them such a unique identity and vision that they were worth top dollar, or (b) the entirely untethered environment created chaos that could only be fixed through the sale to TBWA. TBWA/Chiat/Day built yet another striking—if far more territorial—facility in California to the designs of Frank Gehry alumnus Clive Wilkinson who has also built new quarters for the company's New York offices.

Chiat's approach, however, has proved influential. Teamwork spaces dedicated to particular clients or products have now become commonplace in advertising.[33]

Projects like Chiat/Day simply recognize that the nature of work is becoming more mobile and fluid. Alfred P. West, president of SEI Investments in Oaks, Pennsylvania, found himself reconfiguring teams so often that he and his architect, Meyer, Scherer & Rockcastle, simply put everyone's desk on wheels and plugged them into a reconfigurable power, data, and telecommunications network dangling from the ceiling.[34]

By the late 1990s, Jonathan Ryburg was able to document a broad movement in restructuring American businesses toward a "high-context" work culture of frequent meetings, greater socialization, and lowered hierarchies, emblematic of the urban cultures of Italy, Spain, and Japan. (His Facilities Performance Group of Ann Arbor, Michigan, analyzes changing work patterns.) Northern Europe retained its "low-context" approach (emulating the sociology of England and Germany) of private offices and closed doors.[35]

## coffee bar culture comes to the valley

Changing the fundamental American culture of work has not been easy, nor was it initially clear that architecture could help business evolve. The high-risk, high-reward culture of Silicon Valley, however, has proved a strangely fertile field for workplace transformation through architecture.

In only forty years, according to *Business Week,* the orchards that once dotted the flatlands stretching forty miles along the southwestern edge of San Francisco Bay have been replaced by a conurbation of computer hardware and software companies whose combined $450 billion market value dwarfed that of Hollywood and Detroit in 1997.[36] It is safe to

**Young & Rubicam "Theatre of the Brand" space,** 2000; Los Angeles, California; Designer: Haworth Ideation Team; Courtesy Haworth

**SEI Investments headquarters,**
1997; Oaks, Pennsylvania;
Architect: Meyer, Scherer &
Rockcastle; Photographer:
© Timothy Hursley,
The Arkansas Office, Inc.

**Apple Advanced Computer
Technology Center,** 1986;
Cupertino, California;
Architect: Studios Architecture;
Photographer: © Paul Warchol
Photography, Inc.

say that the valuations of these publicly held companies have at least doubled since then.

This enormous wealth creation did not occur in an environment friendly to architecture. The titans of the high-tech era conducted a decades-long love affair with the lowly garage. In 1939, William Hewlett and David Packard founded their company in a Palo Alto garage with a $538 loan from their electronics teacher at Stanford University. The first Apple computer was built by Steve Jobs and Steve Wozniak in yet another Palo Alto garage. Many know of MIT's Building 20, which retained its legendary status as an incubator of innovative ideas for decades after its first intended date with the wrecking ball.[37] The building met its ultimate demise in March, 1999.

As the personal-computer industry exploded from tiny roots in dingy spaces, the garage paradigm took on the glow of creation myth. As these firms grew, they wanted to hold on to the fever of that nothing-to-lose startup era. So they built bigger garages. Architecture, as traditionally practiced, seemed to offer little when getting hundreds of thousands of raw square feet ready for occupancy as quickly as possible was, for so many companies, struggle enough.

But a funny thing happened on the way to the initial public offering. These companies learned that it is hard to keep a daredevil, risk-taking culture alive once thousands and not dozens of employees are bent to the task of finding the Next Big Thing—which, by the way, has to be rolled out in eighteen months. By the mid-1990s, the computer industry found itself in the vicelike grip of a new range of competitive challenges. To get products into the marketplace at unprecedented speed, they recognized that they had to manage the incubation of ideas, inducing normally solitary engineers to work efficiently together in giant teams. Further, the companies had to work harder to retain valued

staffers, who found jobs aplenty within two to three freeway exits.

One architecture firm, Studios Architecture of San Francisco, changed the rules, just as its early client, Apple Computer, with its smiling-face, graphical desktop, transformed the personal computing experience.[38] In a series of interior projects, Studios showed Apple that architecture could reinforce the company's offbeat product-development culture. At the Advanced Computer Technology Center of 1986, a lavender-painted cable tray slipped above rows of workstations, curling up at the end and sliding away under the ceiling. This simple placement of utilitarian trays in a convenient location encouraged software engineers to rewire at will.

Studios helped its clients see that people can't work productively for long in really raw space. They need light, a connection to what's going on in the rest of the world; they need places to interact and to relax. In a 1995 project for Northern Telecom (Nortel), the Canadian telecommunications company, Studios ripped a giant S-shaped corridor out of the middle of three dreary attached warehouses. The corridor created a generous common "street," enabling various departments to see what others were doing. The corridor thrust out of the existing building envelope in a metal- and glass-framed prow—an emblem of the end of the garage-as-workplace era.

More and more companies found themselves betting very large numbers of people and a great deal of money on unproved ideas—and then doing it again. "We need 150,000 square feet in twelve months," the fast-growing client might explain. "Oh, and we have no idea who will be in it, or even if we will still need it by then—or if we will need more."

In the 1994 Shoreline Entry Site for Silicon Graphics, Studios departed from the Valley's reflective-glass anonymity to give architectural expression to the culture of heady but treacherous mega-growth. A billboard and recruitment poster, the exterior of the building swept in a long curve along the freeway, punctuated by an oversize, arching entrance canopy.

How did companies not at all used to using architecture come to value it? "In a knowledge economy, what you need is inside people's heads," explained Gene Rae, a Studios principal, in an interview. "People need to be encouraged to find out what they don't know and to share what they do know. We make workspace experiences where these things can happen."[39]

As Studios's clients moved to the stage where they were building half-million-square-foot campuses from scratch, the stakes—and the opportunities—rose. Studios described Silicon Graphics's North Charleston Campus as a kind of high-tech hill town. Its ponds, pools, walkways, towers, and pavilions, shot here and there with second-level futuristic-looking bridges, created an unforgettable identity. Individual buildings were clustered around a central landscaped courtyard, with entrances, stairs, and other common spaces housed in transparent wing-like appendages. But there was an agenda behind the eye-catching architectural gestures and the diverse palette of materials. The very exuberance of the environment fostered loyalty and solidarity, while the strategic scattering of important meeting places and the prominence of circulation gave physical form to the company's idea-sharing and team-focused culture.

The new century ushers in an era of perpetual corporate mutation. Management specialists these days use metaphors derived from nature, describing office ecologies or organic systems. "The knowledge-based organization is a map of very intricate networks," says DEGW's Francis Duffy.[40] "Design studios and theaters are the kinds of metaphors companies will have to use to develop innovative

capabilities," says John Kao, who has taught business creativity at Harvard and Stanford Universities. "You need an environment where you can experiment."[41] Kao has created such an environment in San Francisco, which he calls the Idea Factory. Combining elements of a design studio and a television or multimedia production house, it is a place where businesses can test out means to integrate innovation into processes, whether by assembling expertise in new ways or rapidly prototyping ideas. Workplace analysts foresee only greater fluidity in the use of space. Less of what companies do involves linear processes and fixed jobs with fixed duties. Instead, each new product, each service improvement innovation, becomes a project that is handled by an interdisciplinary team.

Architects and interior designers, who deployed their skills traditionally to denote hierarchy or prestige, have learned to adapt. Now they use spatial drama and architectural materials to signal the youthful, no-holds-barred nature of the workplace, as an advertisement of corporate values, and even as decoration meant to express the nonhierarchical nature of the space. In this topsy-turvy work world, the fitness center or coffee bar gets the most lavish architectural attention.

In a labor-short economy, even windows that open have made a comeback—they are a way of making staff feel valued. For similar reasons, some other environmental innovations pioneered in Europe, such as innovative daylighting and natural ventilation schemes are making a tentative foray into America. The role of architecture as an aid to business is more appreciated than ever, garnering extensive coverage in the business press and inspiring a prominent awards program.[42] (Only Wall Street analysts, like hectoring in-laws, seem unhappy with the union, questioning the utility of any but lowest-common-denominator design in growth-company facilities.)

**Northern Telecom (Nortel),** 1996;
Santa Clara, California;
Architect: Studios Architecture;
Photographer: © Michael O'Callahan

**Silicon Graphics, Shoreline
Entry Site,** 1994;
Mountain View, California;
Architect: Studios Architecture;
Photographer: © Paul Warchol
Photography, Inc.

Indeed, office-design culture is today so volatile that yet a new direction manifested itself early in 2000. A new Gold Rush is happening on the construction-clogged streets of San Francisco's once decrepit South of Market neighborhood, driven by the billion-dollar dreams of "new economy" Internet entrepreneurs and the open wallets of venture capitalists. Rechristened Multimedia Gulch, developers and architects cannot convert the former garages, factories, and lofts quickly enough to accommodate companies which months earlier may not have existed.

Internet-startup clients are changing the rules in several respects. They are heavy on graphic designers, interface designers, and animators, people whose education may be art school, whose lifestyle is urban, who draw inspiration from arts and culture, and who socialize in downtown nightclubs rather than suburban golf clubs. They tend to prefer urban loft environments to the carpeted, mirror-glass confines of office parks. Web-oriented businesses have tied up nearly all the available loft space in Chicago's Loop and in New York's "Silicon Alley." Loft structures in the echoing emptiness of downtown Detroit now flicker with lights late at night—a mini-revival driven by the dot-com boom.

Because of the design-driven nature of such businesses, architecture is playing a much more important role, shaping distinctive cultures and images for many of these companies. Some architects are even devising new dot-com prototypes. It's a heady moment. Architecture, at last, may play the role it has always sought: putting a face on the creation and sharing of knowledge; creating an experiential environment that can alter and be altered by shape-shifting business.

Or the moment could evanesce, just, as many predict, the "new economy" will.

**Silicon Graphics, North Charleston Campus,** 1997; Mountain View, California; Architect: Studios Architecture; Photographer: © Richard Barnes

1. Samuel Haber, *Efficiency and Uplift: Scientific Management in the Progressive Era, 1880-1920* (Chicago: University of Chicago Press, 1964), 18–19.

2. Jack Quinan, *Frank Lloyd Wright's Larkin Building: Myth and Fact* (New York: Architectural History Foundation and MIT Press, 1987).

3. Ibid., ch. 4.

4. Ibid., 100.

5. Haber, *Efficiency and Uplift*, 19.

6. Sudhir Kakar, *Frederick Taylor: A Study in Personality and Innovation* (Cambridge, Mass.: MIT Press, 1970), 18.

7. Frederick W. Taylor, *The Principles of Scientific Management* (New York: Harper & Brothers, 1911).

8. Haber, *Efficiency and Uplift*, 53.

9. Ibid., 24.

10. Ibid., 5, and Kakar, *Frederick Taylor*, 19.

11. Haber, *Efficiency and Uplift*, 84.

12. Herbert Croly, *The Promise of American Life* (New York: Macmillan, 1909).

13. Haber, *Efficiency and Uplift*, 141.

14. Eric Sundstrom, *Work Places: The Psychology of the Physical Environment in Offices and Factories* (New York: Cambridge University Press, 1986), 44.

15. "The Army's Pentagon Building," *Architectural Record* 93 (January 1942): 66 and (January 1943): 63–67.

16. Stewart Brand, *How Buildings Learn* (New York: Viking, 1994), 25–27.

17. James S. Russell, "Emblems of Modernism or Machine-Age Dinosaurs?" *Architectural Record* 177 (June 1989): 142–47.

18. Theorist and critic Reyner Bahnham celebrated the expressive elegance of building-systems technology in his seminal history, *The Architecture of the Well-Tempered Environment* (Chicago: University of Chicago Press, 1969).

19. William H. Whyte, *The Organization Man* (New York: Simon & Schuster, 1956)

20. R.H. Shreve, "The Empire State Building Organization," *Architectural Forum* 52 (June 1930): 771.

21. Sundstrom, *Work Places*, 36, citing Lila Shoshkes, *Space Planning: Designing the Office Environment* (New York: Architectural Record Books, 1976).

22. Reinhold Hohl, *Office Buildings: An International Survey* (New York: Praeger, 1968), 56–61.

23. John Pile, "The Nature of Office Landscaping," *AIA Journal* 52 (July 1969): 40–48. See also "Brolandschaft USA," *Progressive Architecture* 49 (May 1968): 174–77.

24. Ibid.

25. Francis Duffy, *The New Office* (London: Conran Octopus, 1997), 36–37.

26. Gabriele Bramante, *Foster Associates: Willis, Faber & Dumas Building, Ipswich, 1975*. Architecture in Detail series published by Phaidon, repackaged as *Architecture 3s: Pioneering British 'High Tech.'* London: Phaidon, 1999.

27. Duffy, *New Office*, 12–18, supported by numerous interviews with Duffy and others by author.

28. Colin Davies, "Machine for Governing," *Architecture* 83 (September 1994): 74–78 and Hugh Aldersey-Williams, "Streamlined Government," *Architectural Record* 80 (June 1992): 96–99.

29. Mary Pepchinski, "With Its Naturally Ventilated Skin and Gardens in the Sky, Foster and Partners' Commerzbank Reinvents the Skyscraper," *Architectural Record* 186 (January 1998): 69–79 and Tracy Metz, "The New Downtown," *Architectural Record* 180 (June 1992): 80–83.

30. Tom Peters and Robert H. Waterman, *In Search of Excellence: Lessons from America's Best-Run Corporations* (New York: Warner Books, 1982); Richard C. Whitely, *The Customer-Driven Company* (New York: Addison-Wesley, 1991); Michael Hammer and James Champy, *Reengineering the Corporation* (New York: HarperBusiness, 1993). This list is hardly exhaustive.

31. *The Impact of Office Environment on Productivity and Quality of Working Life* (Buffalo, N.Y.: BOSTI, 1981); Franklin Becker and Fritz Steele, *Workplace by Design: Mapping the High-Performance Workscape* (San Francisco: Jossey-Bass, 1995); Duffy, *New Office*. The cited authors have written numerous books, studies, and articles on the subject.

32. Karin Tetlow, "Virtually Brave New World," *Architectural Record* (September 1994): 88–97. Coverage of McCaw Communications, Kirkland, Wa.; Ernst & Young offices in Chicago and New York City; Chiat/Day Advertising offices in New York and Los Angeles.

33. Ibid.; also Mildred Friedman, ed., *Gehry Talks: Architecture and Process* (New York, Rizzoli, 1999), 66–71. A critical view of Chiat/Day was written by Warren Berger, "Lost in Space," *Wired* 7 (February 1999). Chiat defended himself in an interview with the author, June 1999. The new Chiat/Day Los Angeles offices are discussed in Clifford Pearson, "After Trying the Virtual, Clive Wilkinson Gets Real with New Offices for TBWA/Chiat/Day," *Architectural Record* 187 (August 1999): 102–07.

34. James S. Russell, "A Company Headquarters Planned for Flexibility," *New York Times*, 7 September 1998.

35. Author interview, August 1997.

36. *Business Week* 3541 (August 25, 1997): 66.

37. Brand, *How Buildings Learn*, 29.

38. Projects discussed are all shown in the monograph *Studios Architecture: The Power of the Pragmatic* (Milan: L'Arca Edizioni, 1999). See also Aaron Betsky, "Agile Architecture," *Architectural Record* 184 (May 1996): 72–79 (Silicon Graphics Entry Site); Aaron Betsky, "Boxes with a Twist," *Architectural Record* 184 (December 1996): 40–43 (Northern Telecom); and Cathy Lang Ho, "Silicon Graphics, Mountain View, California," *Architectural Record* 186 (June 1998): 154–58 (North Charleston Site). Quotations from Studios principals are from author interviews.

39. Author interview, February 2000.

40. Author interview, April 1998.

41. Author interview, April 1998.

42. Since 1997, *Business Week* has cosponsored a design awards program with *Architectural Record* and the American Institute of Architects. The contest recognizes architecture that helps companies do business better.

# time and motion

The mechanization of the office by technologies such as typewriters and computers has paralleled American businesses' attempts to make office workers function with machinelike precision. Throughout the 1910s, time-and-motion studies applied the assembly-line techniques of the automobile industry to the office. Later, ergonomic studies quantified human measurements, posture, and reach in order to establish standards for office furniture and equipment. "Office Supplies" charts the emergence of modular furniture systems from this research. In other efforts to promote good management and efficiency, manuals and advertisements counseled office workers on proper behavior and dress, establishing an office culture of regimentation and conformity.

—D.A., C.B.B.

**Margaret Owen in a time-and-motion typing study by Frank Gilberth,** 1916; Remington Typewriter Company, Ilion, New York; Courtesy Gilbreth Collection, National Museum of American History

**Typewriter,** 1950s; Courtesy Ewing Galloway

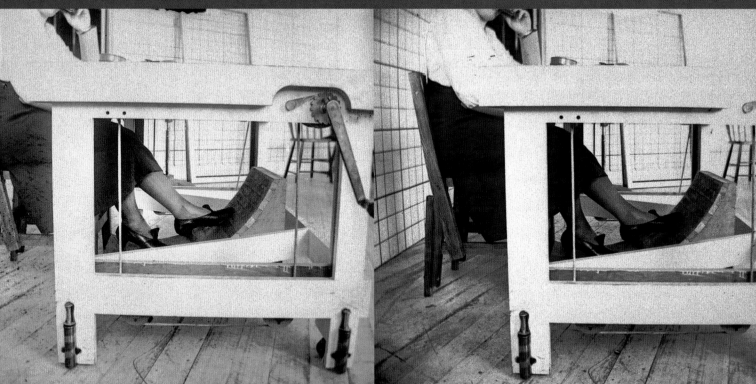

**Stereoscopic image of ideal foot placement for productive work,** 1917; Courtesy Gilbreth Collection, National Museum of American History

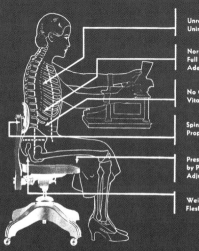

Unrestricted Heart Action. Unimpeded Blood Flow.

Normal Lung Capacity. Full Breathing. Adequate Oxygen.

No Cramping of Vital Organs.

Spinal Column Properly Supported.

Pressure Removed by Proper Design and Adjustment of Seat.

Weight Carried on Fleshy Part of Thighs.

**Advertising graphic for the GF Goodform posture chair from the General Fireproofing Company Metal Office Equipment Catalog,** c. 1936; Courtesy Warshaw Collection, Archives Center, National Museum of American History

**Typing pool at the Equitable Assurance Company,** 1934; New York, New York; Courtesy Peter A. Juley & Son Collection, National Museum of American History

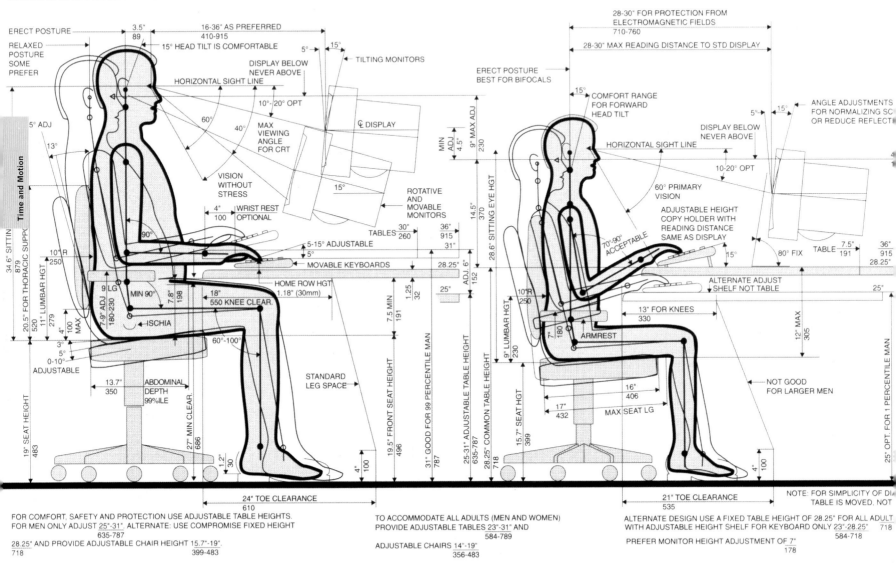

# LARGE MAN 99 PERCENTILE US POPULATION

# SMALL MAN 1 PERCENTILE US POPULATION

ERECT POSTURE

RELAXED POSTURE SOME PREFER

3.5"
89

16-36" AS PREFERRED
410-915

15° HEAD TILT IS COMFORTABLE

DISPLAY BELOW NEVER ABOVE

HORIZONTAL SIGHT LINE

5°

15°

TILTING MONITORS

5° ADJ

13°

10°-20° OPT

60°

40°

MAX VIEWING ANGLE FOR CRT

Ȼ DISPLAY

VISION WITHOUT STRESS

15°

ROTATIVE AND MOVABLE MONITORS

**Time and Motion**

4"
100

WRIST REST OPTIONAL

TABLES
30"
260

36"
915

90°

10° R
250

5-15° ADJUSTABLE

31"

5°

MOVABLE KEYBOARDS

28.25"

34.6" SITTING
879

20.5" FOR THORACIC SUPP

11" LUMBAR HGT
279

9 LG

MIN 90°

7.8"
198

18"

HOME ROW HGT
1.18" (30mm)

550 KNEE CLEAR.

7.5 MIN
191

1.25"
32

25"

7-9" ADJ
180-230

4"
100

MAX

ISCHIA

SITTING EYE HGT

ADJ. 6"
152

3°

5°

0-10°
ADJUSTABLE

60°-100°

13.7"
350

ABDOMINAL DEPTH 99%ILE

STANDARD LEG SPACE

27" MIN CLEAR.
686

19" SEAT HEIGHT
483

1.2"
30

19.5" FRONT SEAT HEIGHT
496

31" GOOD FOR 99 PERCENTILE MAN
787

25-31" ADJUSTABLE TABLE HEIGHT
635-787

28.25" COMMON TABLE HEIGHT
718

4"
100

24" TOE CLEARANCE
610

28-30" FOR PROTECTION FROM ELECTROMAGNETIC FIELDS
710-760

28-30" MAX READING DISTANCE TO STD DISPLAY

ERECT POSTURE BEST FOR BIFOCALS

15°

COMFORT RANGE FOR FORWARD HEAD TILT

ANGLE ADJUSTMENTS FOR NORMALIZING SC OR REDUCE REFLECT

MIN ADJ 4.5"

9" MAX ADJ
230

DISPLAY BELOW NEVER ABOVE

HORIZONTAL SIGHT LINE

5°

15°

10-20° OPT

14.5"
370

60° PRIMARY VISION

ADJUSTABLE HEIGHT COPY HOLDER WITH READING DISTANCE SAME AS DISPLAY

70°-90° ACCEPTABLE

15°

80° FIX

TABLE
7.5"
191

36"
915

28.25"

28.6" SITTING EYE HGT

ALTERNATE ADJUST SHELF NOT TABLE

25"

10° R
250

9" LUMBAR HGT
230

7"
180

ARMREST

13" FOR KNEES
330

12" MAX
305

17"
432

16"
406

MAX SEAT LG

NOT GOOD FOR LARGER MEN

15.7" SEAT HGT
399

25" OPT. FOR 1 PERCENTILE MAN

4"
100

21" TOE CLEARANCE
535

NOTE: FOR SIMPLICITY OF DI TABLE IS MOVED. NOT

FOR COMFORT, SAFETY AND PROTECTION USE ADJUSTABLE TABLE HEIGHTS.
FOR MEN ONLY ADJUST <u>25"-31"</u>. ALTERNATE: USE COMPROMISE FIXED HEIGHT
635-787
<u>28.25"</u> AND PROVIDE ADJUSTABLE CHAIR HEIGHT <u>15.7"-19"</u>.
718
399-483

TO ACCOMMODATE ALL ADULTS (MEN AND WOMEN)
PROVIDE ADJUSTABLE TABLES <u>23"-31"</u> AND
584-789

ADJUSTABLE CHAIRS <u>14"-19"</u>
356-483

ALTERNATE DESIGN USE A FIXED TABLE HEIGHT OF 28.25" FOR ALL ADULT
WITH ADJUSTABLE HEIGHT SHELF FOR KEYBOARD ONLY <u>23"-28.25"</u>   718
584-718

PREFER MONITOR HEIGHT ADJUSTMENT OF <u>7"</u>
178

**Computer stations study from** *The Measure of Man & Woman: Human Factors in Design*, 1993; Authors: Alvin R. Tilley and Henry Dreyfuss Associates;

© 1993 by Whitney Library of Design; Published by Whitney Library of Design, an imprint of Watson-Guptill Publications, New York.

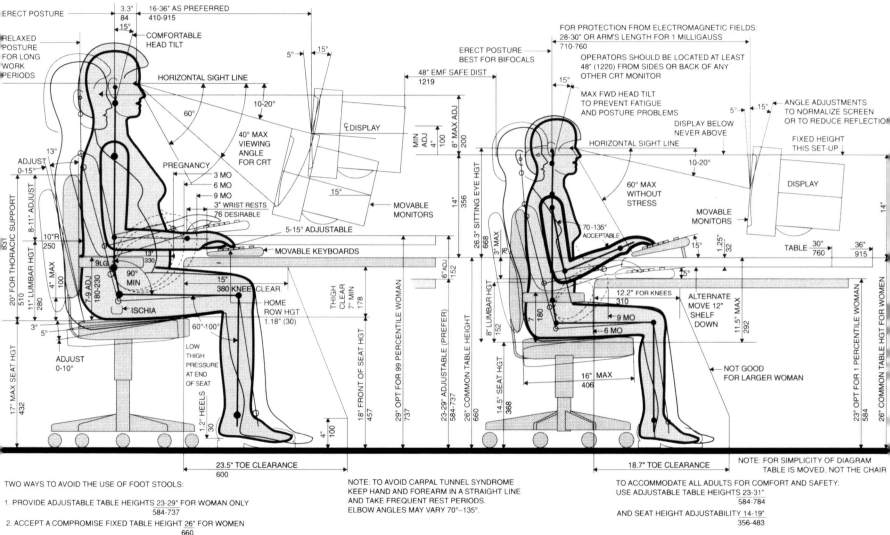

TWO WAYS TO AVOID THE USE OF FOOT STOOLS:

1. PROVIDE ADJUSTABLE TABLE HEIGHTS 23-29" FOR WOMAN ONLY
584-737

2. ACCEPT A COMPROMISE FIXED TABLE HEIGHT 26" FOR WOMEN
660
NOTE: NOT GOOD FOR MOUSE IF TABLE IS ABOVE ELBOW

NOTE: TO AVOID CARPAL TUNNEL SYNDROME
KEEP HAND AND FOREARM IN A STRAIGHT LINE
AND TAKE FREQUENT REST PERIODS.
ELBOW ANGLES MAY VARY 70°–135°.

TO ACCOMMODATE ALL ADULTS FOR COMFORT AND SAFETY:
USE ADJUSTABLE TABLE HEIGHTS 23-31"
584-784
AND SEAT HEIGHT ADJUSTABILITY 14-19"
356-483

NOTE: FOR SIMPLICITY OF DIAGRAM
TABLE IS MOVED, NOT THE CHAIR

Typical office floor, Union
Carbide Building, 1960;
New York, New York;
Architect: Skidmore, Owings &
Merrill; Photographer:
Ezra Stoller © Esto

# office supplies

## evolving furniture for the evolving workplace

Stanley Abercrombie

**Typical office floor, Prudential Building,** 1960s; Newark, New Jersey; Courtesy Prudential Insurance Company of America

Prudential's offices were a vernacular version of Union Carbide's high-style headquarters, without the benefit of Skidmore, Owings & Merrill's visual sophistication and commitment to total design.

It was different, we're told, in the Garden of Eden. Ever since, it has been our lot to work. At first we worked independently, scraping together the necessities for ourselves and our families, then later, more cooperatively, pursuing our specialties and bartering the results. These specialties have often been confined to specific sites, beginning outside with the garden plot, the farmyard, the mine, and the fishing boat, and then coming inside to the workbench, the potter's wheel, the blacksmith's anvil, the loom, and the drafting table. This essay is the story of one group of specialists—office workers—and how they have interacted with their work sites.

We know them well. Few of us have escaped a period in our lives devoted to work in an office, and the dominance in our culture of office work has been an established fact for generations, as has the dominance of our skylines by the office tower that symbolizes such work—a building type that American sociologist C. Wright Mills has called an "enormous file." Remarkably close to us in time, however, are the notions that such work should be—or even could be—made better and more pleasant by alterations in the office itself.

Two ideas are involved. The first is that the office might be changed for the better by the application of artistic principles. This is an idea that first gained widespread credibility in the nineteenth century, when it was imagined that even something as gritty, varied, and unwieldy as a nineteenth-century city could be made beautiful. Art, it had come to be thought, could descend from the easel and pedestal to take part in everyday life.

Ralph Waldo Emerson was a prophet of the idea of applied art. In his 1841 essay "Art," he wrote that "the distinction between the fine and the useful arts [must] be forgotten. . . . In nature all is useful, all is beautiful. It is therefore beautiful because it is alive, moving, reproductive; it is therefore useful because it is symmetrical and fair. . . . It is in vain that we look for genius to reiterate its miracles in the old arts; it is its instinct to find beauty and holiness in new and necessary facts, in the field and roadside, in the shop and mill."[1] And, he might have added, in the office.

The second idea is that office improvement could result from the application of the principles of mechanical efficiency not only to machines but also to machine operators. That idea had a prophet as well, the Philadelphia engineer, steelworker, and inventor Frederick W. Taylor. In 1903, Taylor published an article in the *Transactions of the American Society of Mechanical Engineers*,[2] which he expanded into the widely read 1911 book, *The Principles of Scientific Management*. Rather than treating the worker as a machine, as some oversimplifications of "Taylorism" did, Taylor's writings recognized the worker as an integral and significant part of the work process and mandated layouts and conditions supporting productivity. The process indeed involved time-and-motion studies, but their eventual goal was a democratic, not an autocratic one—in Taylor's own words, the "development of each man to his greatest efficiency and prosperity."[3]

What remained was to synthesize these two ideas and to apply the synthesis to the office and its equipment. The more beautiful and better-furnished office was found to promote the greater efficiency; the more efficient was judged the more attractive. Such a linkage of form and function is at least as old as Socrates, who (in Edgar Cardew Marchant's translation of Xenophon's *Memorabilia and Oeconomicus*) says that a dung basket is beautiful and a golden shield ugly "if the one is well made for its special work and the other badly."[4] But this linkage became a powerful article of faith for the designers of early modernism. For Frank Lloyd Wright, particularly, a work of architecture, at its best, was a single organism, with all its parts related in a functional way and its beauty derived from that organic interconnection. An example was the first great office interior of the twentieth century, Wright's 1906 Larkin Administration Building in Buffalo, New York.

Wright's achievement cannot be fully appreciated without a reminder of the context from which it exploded. The contrast is immense, yet earlier attempts at office furniture—even while the office was still often at home, without phones or typewriters, without even an inkling of faxes and computers—were far from ludicrous. Even the most decorous examples, such as an eighteenth-century writing table by Chippendale, demonstrate a trend that the twentieth century pursued with vigor: the provision of a complete ensemble of writing surface and varied storage compartments for writing and business supplies. Mr. Chippendale's table, no less than the latest office system, was multifunctional.

A century later, the writing table had grown larger and more complex. The most heroic of all the Victorian desks, one truly architectural in scope, was the Wooton desk, made by W.S. Wooton of Indianapolis beginning around 1874. A monster composed of three hinged parts, it virtually enveloped its user and offered dozens of shelves, pigeonholes, and drawers, not to mention a pediment and finials.

Wright, of course, would have none of this. The Larkin Building centered on a great shaft of space lit from above and from the sides. The desks of executives as well as clerks were at ground level, accessible to the public, while services—such as employee lockers and lunchroom and a precocious system of air ventilation and cooling—were housed in supplemental elements.[5] As Edgar Kaufmann, jr., has written, Wright achieved here "an image of efficiency and human consideration unparalleled in commercial structures of that day."[6]

**Desk with attached, fold-away seat for the Larkin Administration Building,** 1906; Buffalo, New York; Architect and designer: Frank Lloyd Wright; Courtesy Jack Quinan

**Wooton Patent Cabinet Office
Secretary,** c.1880; Courtesy
Oakland Museum of California

**Chippendale writing table,
published in the third edition of
Thomas Chippendale's** *The
Gentleman and Cabinet-Maker's
Director,* 1762; Courtesy the
Winterthur Library: Printed Book
and Periodical Collection

**Great Workroom of the
SC Johnson Administration
Building,** 1939; Racine,
Wisconsin; Architect: Frank
Lloyd Wright; Courtesy
SC Johnson

The building's tapering,
concrete columns, which were
inspired by flowers, resulted in
more office floor space than
would have been possible with a
traditional structural system.
Designed largely without
windows, Wright's masterpiece
used 43 miles of glass tubing
for naturally and artificially lit
skylights, providing shadow-less
illumination.

**Office chair for the SC Johnson
Administration Building,** 1939;
Racine, Wisconsin; Designer: Frank
Lloyd Wright; Manufacturer: Steel-
case; Courtesy SC Johnson

Wright designed the building's
distinctive chairs to complement
the oval desks and the architecture's organic forms. The three-
legged chair tipped over easily if
workers did not sit upright with
both feet on the floor. A fourth leg
was later added for stability.

Wright's furniture for the Larkin Building was an integral part of the organism, designed of riveted planes of sheet steel and fabricated by the Van Dorn Iron Works of Cleveland. Metal file cabinets were built in and cushioned seats were cantilevered from the desks on swivels so they could be folded away for easy cleaning. The cleaning staff, however, may have been more pleased than the office staff—the cantilevered seats allowed limited movement, and some freestanding chairs were designed by Wright with only three legs; easily tipped over, they were dubbed "suicide chairs."[7]

In 1912, the future of manufacturing such equipment was presaged by the founding of the Metal Office Furniture Company in Grand Rapids, Michigan, a city already home to more than sixty furniture companies. Its first products were office safes; two years later it began producing a fireproof steel wastebasket as well. It began making metal desks in 1916, responding to America's burgeoning business culture and capitalizing on the federal government's recent requirement for fireproof furniture in all its new buildings. The company later changed its name to Steelcase, and by 1993 it was the largest furniture manufacturer in the world.

A parallel development in 1923 was the purchase of the eighteen-year-old Michigan Star Furniture Company by an employee, D.J. De Pree. He renamed it Herman Miller in honor of his father-in-law and backer. According to Ralph Caplan's company history, De Pree "began reading books by efficiency experts [presumably including Taylor], an activity interesting in the light of Herman Miller's later involvement in the management of office work."[8]

In 1930, the year that American office space reached a billion square feet, Herman Miller hired New York–based designer Gilbert Rohde, whose relatively uncluttered furniture was consistent with De Pree's ideals of honesty and morality. "With his simplicity," De Pree said, "Rohde had taken away our means of covering up. We had to learn new manufacturing techniques, such as how to make mitered joints in a very precise way."[9]

Rohde was a member of a new breed of business tastemakers—industrial designers—who fashioned modern ideas for design and manufacture. In 1932, Norman Bel Geddes, previously best known as a designer for the theater, created interiors for the New York office of the J. Walter Thompson advertising agency. Two years later, the Metropolitan Museum of Art bestowed its cachet on the whole genre of "streamlined" interiors by reproducing, at full size, the office Raymond Loewy had recently designed for himself.

In 1936, thirty years after the Larkin Building first opened, Frank Lloyd Wright created another innovative office design for the S.C. Johnson Administration Building in Racine, Wisconsin. Its soaring workroom was punctuated with slender "mushroom" columns, with light streaming in through glass tubing between the circular column capitals. As usual, Wright complemented the building with his own interior design and furniture design. The desks handsomely repeated the curves and cantilevers of the surrounding structure and, instead of drawers, featured cylindrical storage bins that swiveled out from under the work surfaces. Unfortunately, some of the seating repeated the three-legged design of the Larkin "suicide chairs," although Wright later relented and added a fourth leg.[10] This time, Wright's furniture designs were manufactured by Steelcase, who subcontracted to Stow & Davis for the racetrack-shaped wood desktops and to American Seating for some tubular steel components.

Rohde's first pieces for Herman Miller were primarily residential but, by 1937, according to company publicity, Rohde had begun "to amend the dissonance between modern office buildings and the furniture available to outfit them." In 1942, Miller introduced Rohde's Executive Office Group, a forerunner of the office systems concept, which offered fifteen components that could be combined in more than four hundred configurations. Bel Geddes and Loewy had been concerned with stylish packaging, but Rohde's provision for easy inter-changeability went deeper than appearance; it shared an interest in modularity with the giants among the early European modernists.

One example was the Casiers Standard group of storage cabinets, designed by Le Corbusier and Pierre Jeanneret and shown at the 1925 Pavilion Ésprit Nouveau in Paris; it was based on a module of 37.5 cm (15 inches). Another, based on a module of 33 cm (13 inches), was developed by Marcel Breuer shortly after he became director of the Bauhaus furniture department in 1924; it appeared in the 1926 Wilensky apartment and the 1927 Piscator apartment, both in Berlin, and in the 1927 Weissenhof Siedlung in Stuttgart. A variant of Breuer's modular cabinetry appeared in his 1929 Harnischmacher office in Mainz, Germany.

Breuer's later furniture—along with the furniture of Ludwig Mies van der Rohe, Harry Bertoia, Jens Risom, Arne Jacobsen, Eero Saarinen, and others—found American champions in German-born Hans Knoll, a Bauhaus enthusiast, and his wife, Florence, a Cranbrook graduate. Knoll International was founded in 1938; the Knoll Planning Unit was added in 1943. Over the next twenty years, Florence Knoll added her own elegant designs to the Knoll collec-tion, including executive desks so spare that, like Breuer's desk for Herr Harnischmacher, they were virtually devoid of storage space.

A forerunner of a different type was the devel-opment by George Nelson and Henry Wright of a notion they called the Storagewall. It appeared in their 1945 bestseller *Tomorrow's House* and was popularized by a feature in *Life* magazine.[11] It used a common partition between rooms not as a back-ing for storage elements but as a container of them. The wall itself was put to work—not exactly as architecture, not exactly as furniture, but with qualities of each. Olga Gueft, editor-in-chief of *Interiors* magazine in its heyday, later wrote that "all open plan systems are derived from the possibilities generated by Nelson in that 1945 *Life* spread."

One reader of the *Life* article was D.J. De Pree, who arranged to meet Nelson and hired him soon afterward as Herman Miller's director of design, replacing Rohde, who had unexpectedly died. Nelson, in turn, brought sculptor Isamu Noguchi to Herman Miller as a furniture designer and also insisted that De Pree bring Charles Eames into the firm. "He's doing something I can't do," Nelson told him. In the years to come, of course, Charles and Ray Eames made brilliant contributions to the design of office seating, but not, unfortunately, of other office furniture.

Herman Miller's 1946 collection included designs by both Noguchi and Eames, as well as almost eighty new designs by Nelson. In the 1947 collection, Nelson turned his attention to office work with the Executive Office Group, using the same name as Rohde's earlier design. The heart of the group was an L-shaped desk, but it was more than just a desk; it was "the first example of what came to be called a workstation."[12] Described in the cata-log as a "work center," it combined a writing surface, storage elements (including one for a type-writer), files, and built-in lighting.

The 1950s saw more progress in the design of office buildings than in the design of what might furnish them. The two most notable office structures were—in the early 1950s—Lever House by Gordon Bunshaft of Skidmore, Owings & Merrill and—in the late 1950s—the Seagram Building by Ludwig Mies van der Rohe.

**Storagewall concept by George Nelson and Henry Wright,** published in *Life*, January 22, 1945; Courtesy George Nelson Archives, Vitra Design Museum, Weil am Rhein

**George Nelson's 1947
Executive Office Group;**
Courtesy Herman Miller

**Harnischmacher office with
modular storage units,** 1929;
Mainz, Germany;
Architect: Marcel Breuer;
Courtesy the Museum of
Modern Art, New York

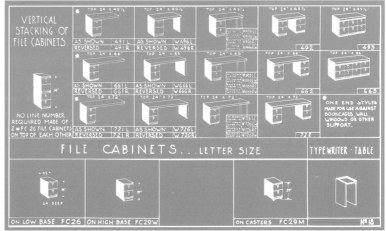

**Promotional graphic (detail) of
Gilbert Rohde's 1942 Executive
Office Group;** Courtesy Herman Miller

## caves    commons

|  | **caves** | **commons** |
|---|---|---|
| *getting work done* | Private offices are quiet places for creative thinking. | Working in wide-open spaces enhances interaction with others. |
| *networking* | Talking with fellow workers is easy through phone or email. | You're out in the open, in full view and easy reach of everyone. |
| *who's the boss* | The bigger the private office and more expensive the finishes, the more important you are. | Status is "old economy." |
| *office culture* | We value an individual's privacy. | We're one big, happy family. |
| *design* | You may hang up as many family snapshots and mementos as you wish. | You must follow guidelines that work within the office's design. |

Offices may be divided into "caves" (private offices) or "commons" (communal spaces). Both concepts have their proponents.

**Advertising photograph for Herman Miller's 1964 Action Office;** Designer: George Nelson and Robert Propst; Courtesy George Nelson Archives, Vitra Design Museum Archives, Weil am Rhein

**Advertising photograph for
Action Office II,** 1968;
Designer: Robert Propst;
Courtesy Herman Miller

Not until 1960, however, was there an integration of this new architecture with new interiors and new furniture design that could begin to match Wright's 1906 synthesis in the Larkin Administration Building. The new example was on Park Avenue in New York, just south of Lever and Seagram: the Union Carbide Building by Skidmore, Owings & Merrill. It triumphantly fulfilled the modular dreams of Breuer, Le Corbusier, and Rohde. Union Carbide's structural system, its fenestration, its luminous plastic ceiling panels, its metal partitions, its filing cabinets, and its desks—all these were ordered by a single module of thirty inches. It may once have occurred to the designers that only sixty-inch-tall workers should be employed, but some exceptions to the module were finally allowed. Union Carbide was the expression of an ideal to an extreme degree that would never be repeated. Whatever its practical shortcomings, it was indisputably thorough.

The universal order of Union Carbide was based on universal certainties about the nature of office work. Within the next few years, however, those certainties were challenged, first by a young inventor from Colorado, then by two brothers from a suburb of Hamburg, Germany.

The inventor, Robert Propst, spent his time imagining new types of heart valves, playground equipment, and livestock tagging machines until 1960, when Herman Miller established the Herman Miller Research Corporation in Ann Arbor, Michigan, and appointed Propst its first director. Propst then turned his attention to the office. The Research Corporation assembled a lengthy questionnaire and sent it to office workers. "Who can overhear your phone conversation?" it asked. "Can you take a nap in your office without embarrassment? Can you keep your papers visibly available?" The answers led Propst to an assortment of notions about the office, such as "people like to support their extremities," "body motion" is related to "mental fluency," and deep drawers become "vertical paper bottlenecks."[13]

Interesting, but hardly marketable. George Nelson was asked to make Propst's ideas manifest in an actual product line and, after much collaboration by the two, Herman Miller introduced the first version of Action Office in 1964. Cantilevered from die-cast aluminum legs, the rubber-edged desks had plastic-laminate work surfaces that could be covered at night with a roll of canvas or a wood tambour. The accompanying seat was not a chair but a tall, narrow perch; other elements included a movable storage unit and a sound-insulated "communications center" for telephone and Dictaphone use. The design was seen as revolutionary, and it generated enormous publicity in the business and general press as well as in the design magazines.[14] Unfortunately, the reception in the press was more positive than the reception in the showrooms. American workers and managers were apparently unwilling to trade their familiar mahogany desks for strange blue (or green or yellow) objects on shiny legs. Action Office was a succés d'estime, but not a financial success.

At the same time, in Quickborn, Germany, brothers Eberhard and Wolfgang Schnelle, partners in a management consulting firm, were developing their own radical notion: that the arrangement of office furniture should be planned not according to rank or organization charts but patterns of communication among workers. The visual implication of this notion, which they called *bürolandschaft* ("office landscape"), was that the orderly rows of desks prevailing in virtually every office previously conceived were swept away; in their place were apparently random clusters of furniture separated by empty spaces, screens, and potted plants. The Quickborner team's first U.S. commission was a floor for the Freon Products Division of Du Pont in Wilmington, Delaware (1967). On other floors of the same building, Du Pont provided more conventional layouts with ceiling-height partitions, and department managers were invited to observe the Quickborner experiment. None, it seems, chose "office landscape" for their own departments, but—like Action Office—it attracted much favorable attention. *Progressive Architecture* magazine described it as "an open, unenclosed space with activities swirling to diffusion" and predicted that "office landscape will, incontestably, become firmly rooted."[15]

The Quickborner Team claimed that their vision required no specially designed equipment, and the Wilmington space was, indeed, furnished with stock items. Even so, it was clear that the vision would be most successful if its furniture were interchangeable, lightweight, and easily reconfigured. Herman Miller went to work—with Propst but without Nelson—to make Action Office more popular, and Action Office II appeared in 1968. In the design, Quickborner's desks and screens were united, and work surfaces and storage units were hung from the movable panels.

Others went to work as well: In 1969, Ettore Sottsass Jr. designed the Sistema 45 for Olivetti and Douglas Ball designed the S System steel desk. In 1970, Otto Zapf designed the Softline System for Knoll and William Pulgram developed the TRM (task response module) System for Eppinger.

Perhaps the most handsome of the new rash of furniture systems was developed for the 300,000 square feet of "office landscape" space in the new headquarters designed by Skidmore, Owings & Merrill for the Weyerhauser Corporation in Tacoma, Washington. Its design was a collaboration of SOM's Charles Pfister (working under SOM design partner Edward C. Bassett) and Bill Stephens of Knoll's Design and Development Group. The system's interlocking panels offered an impression of sturdiness and the warmth of wood, and Knoll began marketing it in 1971 as the Stephens System.

The same year, Steelcase introduced Movable Walls, its first comprehensive systems furniture line. The system's basic element was a bit like Nelson and Wright's Storagewall on casters. In 1972, Knoll's accomplishments in both office and residential furniture were recognized in a retrospective exhibition at the Louvre. The following year, Haworth, founded in 1948 as Modern Products, introduced Modern Office Modules (nicknamed "Mom"), its first office furniture product.

In 1975, Nelson himself was back on the leading edge of systems furniture design with his eponymous Nelson Workspaces for the Canadian manufacturer Storwal. Nelson based Workspaces on the philosophy that workers' contentment and efficiency could be fostered by augmenting their ability to make individual adjustments to their own environments. The basic element of Workspaces was a desk on which could be stacked selected components—rather than walls from which components were hung—including bookshelves, planter boxes, and filler panels with glass and little venetian blinds that allowed workers to control their privacy.

A less ingratiating but more fundamental step was taken by Haworth in 1976 with the introduction of ERA-1, the first prewired modular office panel. From that date, office furniture also became a power source. In 1985, however, Haworth sued Steelcase for patent infringement involving wired panels. The suit was settled in 1996 with a $211.5 million award for Haworth. Whatever the merits of the opposing arguments, it was clearly determined that Haworth had had a valuable idea.

In the late 1970s and throughout the 1980s, office systems proliferated like wildflowers, many of them indistinguishable from each other. In 1984, *Arts & Architecture* magazine estimated that there were "over two hundred open office systems on the market."[16] Most notable among these were Sunar's

**Stephens System office furnishings, originally designed for Weyerhauser headquarters,** 1971; Tacoma, Washington; Designer: Knoll International with Skidmore, Owings & Merrill; Photographer: Ezra Stoller © Esto

**Open office landscape at S.I. Du Pont's Freon Products Division,** 1967; Wilmington, Delaware; Planner: Quickborner Team; Courtesy *Open Office Planning* by John Pile, © 1978 by Whitney Library of Design; Published by Whitney Library of Design, an imprint of Watson-Guptill Publications, New York.

Movable Walls, Steelcase's
first venture into the office
systems market, 1971;
Courtesy Steelcase

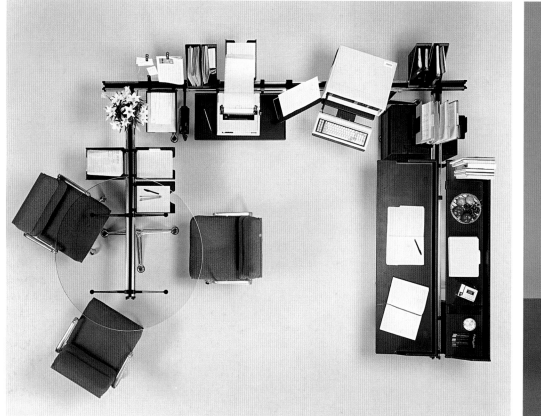

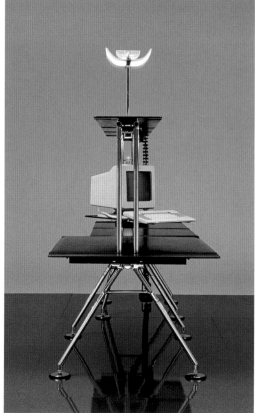

**The 1986 Burdick Group,**
**as photographed in 1992;**
Designer: Bruce Burdick;
Courtesy Herman Miller

**Nomos office furniture system**
**for Tecno,** 1986;
Designer: Foster and Partners;
Photographer: Mauro Masera;
Courtesy Foster and Partners

1978 Race system, by Douglas Ball, which moved the built-in raceway from the panel baseboard to the more convenient desktop height; Herman Miller's 1984 Ethospace system, by Bill Stumpf and Don Chadwick, the first configuration to introduce optional glass panes at the top of the panels; and Herman Miller's 1986 Burdick Group, which made handsome use of glass work surfaces and was capable of many configurations. According to designer Bruce Burdick, the idea of the desk only as a flat surface to write on had become functionally outmoded. "What I wanted was a desk that was responsive to the way an individual works . . . a desk that a designer could specify for 20 different people, with each one being different."[17]

Parallel to and partially guiding this proliferation of systems design were a similar flowering of office seating design and a surge of institutional and governmental interest in the subject. New designs for seating, built on the pioneering designs of the Eameses, were informed by new information about ergonomics. The first attempts at ergonomic seating—before the name was in use—may have been Wright's infamous tripod chairs, for he believed their very insecurity would enforce good posture: sit straight or fall![18] A more scientifically based attempt came in 1976 with Herman Miller's introduction of Bill Stumpf's Ergon chairs. In 1979, Stumpf and Don Chadwick produced the first version of their flexible plastic Equa chair for Herman Miller, and Emilio Ambasz and Giancarlo Piretti their first version of the Vertebra chair for Open Ark.[19] In 1984, Niels Diffrient designed his Helena and Jefferson chairs, both for Sunar Hauserman. Of the many developments since, the one arousing most interest has been Herman Miller's 1994 Aeron chair, another design by Stumpf and Chadwick. Instead of the usual foam and fabric, the Aeron's frame is filled with a pellicle, or thin skin, which adapts to the shape and movement of the occupant. Beneath the seat is a kinemat tilt mechanism that allows the body to pivot naturally.

Government activity affecting office design came as early as 1962, when Congress passed the Revenue Act, which allows a 10 percent investment credit on personal property with a useful life of seven years. Fixed walls, which were considered real estate, couldn't get the credit, but movable panels could. The law undoubtedly had a positive influence (though one difficult to measure) on the proliferation of the new panel systems. In 1970, Congress passed the Occupational Safety and Health Act, which led to the establishment of both NIOSH (the National Institute for Occupational Safety and Health, part of the Department of Health and Human Services) and OSHA (the Occupational Safety and Health Administration, part of the Department of Labor). Both these organizations, and others, affect the overall design of interiors, including furniture and office equipment. Federal regulations establish guidelines, specifications, or minimum standards on a host of topics from lighting, materials, and fabrics to environmental acoustics and physical maladies—like Carpal Tunnel Syndrome, one of many computer-related repetitive-strain injuries.

Institutional activity includes the 1979 founding of the Facility Management Institute as a division of the Herman Miller Research Corporation and, the following year, the formation of the National Facility Management Association, which has been known as the International Facility Management Association since 1983. The International Society of Facilities Executives was established in 1989. All these organizations support the new role of the facility manager, charged with purchasing power as well as the supervision of workplace efficiency, safety, security, and productivity. The simple client-designer relationship of the past is no longer so simple.

**Aeron chair,** 1994; Designer:
Bill Stumpf and Don Chadwick;
Courtesy Herman Miller

A further complication was that the nature of office work continues to change, with more of it being done at home (giving rise to the buzzword "telecommuting"), more of that time being executed on irregular schedules ("flextime"), and more office workstations being available on a temporary basis ("hoteling") rather than permanently assigned to specific employees. A landmark example of interior design for such an "alternate office" was the Switzer Group's 1994 facility in Cranford, New Jersey, providing 180 workspaces for a total of eight hundred "mobile" IBM employees. Monica Geran, writing in *Interior Design*, called it "to date the biggest installation created specifically to conform with changed marketing trends and . . . deploying appropriate space planning and interior design."[20]

Naturally, these facilities demand new types of office equipment, such as personal storage units that can be locked and wheeled to different locations as needed. A compact mobile cabinet was part of Geoff Hollington's 1990 Relay system for Herman Miller; it was called the Puppy. Many of the more recent systems also include such units.

Among the latest systems on the market is Resolve, an open and flexible configuration designed by Ayse Birsel for Herman Miller in 1999, and Haworth's ingeniously simple Crossings Office System of small interlocking tables in the shapes of almost-full moons; the Quickborner Team, one imagines, would have found them ideal for their "office landscape." Important among recent office seating designs are the sleek 1997 Meda chair for Vitra, by Alberto Meda, and the more substantial 1999 Freedom chair, by Niels Diffrient for Humanscale. Ideas further from the mainstream include the Teleport 2.0 of Houston-based architect/educator/futurist Doug Michels, a former member of the iconoclastic Ant Farm group and now on the faculty of the Gerald D. Hines College of Architecture at the University of Houston. An updating of a late 1970s media room, Teleport 2.0 is described as a "cybercraft" and is planned to "produce and receive live Webcasting," perhaps bringing telecommuting to a new level.[21]

What next? The office itself, having dominated our cities, our design, and our lives for most of the twentieth century, may be about to disband. Going to the office is becoming an increasingly rare event, doing our work at home increasingly the norm. The paperless office, long promised, can still become a reality. And our computers become not only more and more indispensable but also more and more invisible. Their keyboards can be replaced by voice recognition, their monitors by a flat wall. The computers themselves can be housed in small compartments of our desks, or on our wrists, or—eventually—in our brains. The office of the future could then become very much like a Chippendale writing table. This is not an entirely unpleasant prospect.

**Resolve Delta workstation configuration**, 1999; Designer: Ayse Birsel for Herman Miller; Courtesy Olive 1:1

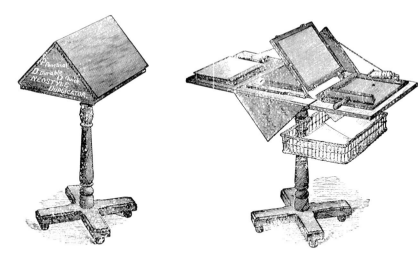

**The Universal Neostyle Duplicator,** c. 1900; Courtesy Warshaw Collection, Archives Center, National Museum of American History

Essentially a personal printing press, this duplicator anticipated today's mobile office furnishings. It featured a revolving ink plate, as well as an automatic self-feeding ink supplier and paper discharge mechanism. Virtually everything could be copied, from a single signature to an entire form.

**"Puppy," a personal mini-office on wheels, part of the Relay System,** 1990; Designer: Geoff Hollington; Courtesy Herman Miller

**Elements of the Crossings Office System,** 1997; Designer: Haworth Ideation Team; Courtesy Haworth

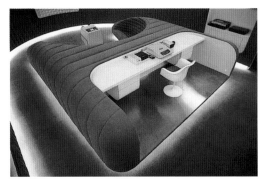

**Allen Teleport, Version 2.0
Cybercraft,** 2000;
Designer: Doug Michels;
Courtesy Doug Michels Studio

**Ford's TH!NK electric car kiosk
at the Detroit Auto Show,** 2000;
Designer: Ford and frogdesign;
Courtesy frogdesign

A truly mobile office, this
version of Ford's electric car
is targeted to corporate and
university campuses in
California and the Sunbelt.
The car includes voice-activated
email, a digital horn that can
be personalized, Internet radio
access, and a global positioning
system. With its swivel seats
and back shelf, the car morphs
into an instant office.

**Steelcase Q workstation
concept,** 1997; Designer:
IDEO for Steelcase;
Courtesy IDEO

An automobile-like furniture
system, the Q workstation
can be driven through the
office. It is powered by a
wheelchair motor and
controlled by a joystick, and
features a seat that rotates
around the structure and a
four-screen display mounted
on a flexible arm.

1. John A. Kouwenhoven, *Made in America: The Arts in Modern Civilization* (1948; reprint, Garden City, N.Y.: Doubleday, 1962), 101.

2. Frederick Winslow Taylor, "Management, Labor Incentives, Wage Problems, and Time and Motion Study," *Transactions of the American Society of Mechanical Engineers* (1903).

3. Kouwenhoven, *Made in America*, 184.

4. Xenophen, "Memorabilia and Oeconomicus," translated by Edgar Cardew Marchant, in *Xenophen: Works*. Volume 4. Loeb Classic Library (1918; reprint, London: W. Heineman, 1968).

5. Although Willis Carrier did not form the Carrier Engineering Corporation until 1915 and did not devise his air-conditioning system for skyscrapers until 1939, he had provided humidity controls for a New York printing plant around 1900. Wright's provision of a system for the Larkin Building is described in Jack Quinan, *Frank Lloyd Wright's Larkin Building: Myth and Fact* (New York and Cambridge: Architectural History Foundation and MIT Press, 1987), 66*ff*.

6. Edgar Kaufmann, jr., "Frank Lloyd Wright," in *Macmillan Encyclopedia of Architects*, vol. 4, ed. Adolf K. Placzek (New York: Free Press, 1982), 437.

7. Quinan, *Frank Lloyd Wright's Larkin Building*, 62.

8. Ralph Caplan, *The Design of Herman Miller* (New York: Whitney Library of Design, 1976).

9. Ibid., 27.

10. Jonathan Lipman, *Frank Lloyd Wright and the Johnson Wax Buildings* (New York: Rizzoli, 1986), 88–89.

11. George Nelson and Henry Wright, *Tomorrow's House* (New York: Simon & Shuster, 1945) and "The Storagewall," *Life* (January 22, 1945).

12. Lance Knobel, *Office Furniture: Twentieth-Century Design* (New York: Dutton, 1987). Similarly, Claude Bunyard called the EOG "possibly the most significant early event in the whole modern office movement" in his article "Office Design in the USA," *Design* 425 (London), (May 1984).

13. "Herman Miller's 'Action Office,'" *Interior Design* 35, no. 12 (December 1964): 34.

14. For example: Mina Hamilton, "Herman Miller in Action," *Industrial Design* 12, no. 1 (January 1965): 26–33; "An Agreeable Office," *Esquire* (December 1964); and "Office Furniture Tailored to the Job," *Business Week*, December 19, 1964. There were also reports in the *New York Times* and *Herald Tribune*, both November 23, 1964.

15. "Office Landscape," *Progressive Architecture* 49, no. 1 (May 1968): 174–77. See also Monica Geran, "Office Landscaping," *Interior Design* 42, no. 5 (May 1971): 110*ff*.

16. Bruno Giberti, "Open Office," *Arts & Architcture* 2, no. 4 (1984).

17. Bruce Burdick, "Change . . . Women Working . . . Skis, Violins, and Desks," *Ideas from Herman Miller* 4, no. 2 (February 1980): 16–19. Other important examples included: Knoll's Zapf system of 1976; Olivetti's 1979 Synthesis system and 1982 Icarus line, both designed by Michele De Lucchi and Ettore Sottsass Jr.; Tecno's 1986 Nomos system by architect Norman Foster; Castelli's 9-to-5 system by Richard Sapper; and Knoll's 1986 Morrison system.

18. Lipman, *Frank Lloyd Wright*, 84–91.

19. The Vertebra chair was later produced by Cassina.

20. Monica Geran, "The Switzer Group," *Interior Design* 65, no. 3 (March 1995): 134–38.

21. Shaila Dawan, "Back to the Futurist," *Houston Press* 11, no. 50 (December 16–22, 1999).

# the paper empire

The office is essentially a factory that produces paper. From the beginnings of modern business culture after the Civil War, new types of jobs, furnishings, and technologies have emerged as ways to improve the processing of paper and the information it contains. As told in "Technology in the Office," the history of the office is the story of standardized paper, envelopes, forms, folders, index cards, and Post-it notes, as well as the specialized furniture and equipment for filing and storing them and machines to duplicate and transmit them. The computer, and its promise of a new way to store information on disks and servers, has been heralded as the key to the "paperless office"—a concept that will likely remain an unfulfilled dream.
—D.A., C.B.B.

**Tradecard, Gordon Step Ladder on Wheels (left),** c.1900; Gordon Traveling Ladder Co., Lexington, Kentucky; Courtesy, Warshaw Collection, Archives Center, National Museum of American History

Specialized office equipment such as this ladder facilitated the growth of office culture. The company offered four ladders, ranging from $10 for a poplar model to $25 for the oak version. Each ladder came with 24 feet of iron-and-wood track.

**Union Mutual employees researching ledger books (facing page left),** c. 1930; Portland, Maine; Photographer: Stuart Wood Hodgdon; Courtesy UnumProvident Corporation

**Open filing system Prudential headquarters (facing page right),** c. 1970; Newark, New Jersey; Courtesy Prudential Insurance Company of America

Desktop computers, which store large quantities of information in small spaces, have largely replaced huge on-site filing rooms, as depicted in this photograph. This shift allows the use of more office space for revenue-generating activities.

**Prudential employees at an off-site storage facility,** c. 1955, Pleasantville, New Jersey. Courtesy Prudential Insurance Company of America

Supplementing its headquarters in Newark, New Jersey, Prudential converted the former Douglass Textile plant into a records retention facility. The transformation of the building's contents from machinery to paper underscored the nation's postwar shift from manufacturing to a service and information economy.

office supplies

tabloid

legal

inter-office envelope

letter

steno pad

A-10 envelope

while you were out

A-7 envelope

#10 envelope

post-it

business card

post-it

United States government filing room, 1939, Washington, D.C.; Photographer: David Myers; Courtesy U.S. Farm Security Administration Collection, Prints and Photographs Division, Library of Congress

Circular filing unit at the
Chesapeake & Potomac Telephone
Company Exchange, c. 1925;
Washington, D.C.;
Photographer: Herbert E. French;
Courtesy National Photo Company
Collection, Prints and Photographs
Division, Library of Congress

**Computer tape storage at Union Mutual headquarters,** c. 1970; Portland, Maine; Courtesy UnumProvident Corporation

**Reconversion in Typewriters,**
*Fortune*, August 1944;
Illustrator: Peter Piening;
Courtesy *Fortune* © 1944 Time
Inc. All rights reserved.

# technology in the office
## individual power and collective standards

Phil Patton

**Thomas Jefferson's desktop polygraph, or copying machine,** c. 1815; Courtesy Special Collections/University of Virginia, Thomas Jefferson Memorial Foundation

This device allowed Jefferson to make a simultaneous copy of any document. Writing with one pen automatically moved the other.

Thomas Jefferson, our most gadget-obsessed president, was particularly fascinated with devices for his office. Having seen his papers destroyed by fire and menaced by invading troops, Jefferson was conscious of the need for governments to preserve copies of documents. He tried several versions of the pantograph, a mechanical tool that made copies of pen-written documents, and regularly used a copying press, a primitive form of carbon paper.

Jefferson's letters, says Silvio A. Bedini in *Thomas Jefferson and His Copying Machines*, are full of notes on testing such duplicating devices as the Hawkins and Peale Patent Polygraph, Ralph Wedgewood's Pennapolygraph, and the Manifold Stylographic Writer. He even devised portable desks to contain his favorite writing tools, from sealing wax to pens. (Jefferson owned one of the earliest fountain pens.) From rotating desk chairs and book holders to the portable writing desk on which he drafted the Declaration of Independence, Jefferson's office

tools were the products of decades of experimentation born of an Enlightenment optimism. Today, Jefferson's devices are mostly footnotes to office history. However, his fascination prefigured a wider American belief that office tools could produce greater efficiencies and magnify the power of the individual.

Our common vision of ourselves, in the office as in the laboratory and factory, is Jeffersonian: We think of ourselves as a country of independent tinkerers, harvesting ideas and technologies, much as Jefferson idealized us as a nation of independent farmers. The America that creates new inventions in barns or garages, then turns them into huge industries, is a vision alive and well in twenty-first-century Silicon Valley.

But "growing technologies" has been only part of the tale. The reality is as much Hamiltonian as Jeffersonian. The birth of invention and industry and the evolution of office technology shows an

important role for government investment and infrastructure, for the power of shared standards over individual innovations. Technology's impact on the office, as on other spheres of life, has always been tempered by social and cultural factors, some resisting, some furthering innovation, and always torn between individual power and collective connection.

The arrival of machines in the office—the mechanical calculator, the address machine, the check writer—came as office planners and executives aspired to achieve for office work the results time-and-motion-study guru Frederick W. Taylor was bringing to manufacturing early in the twentieth century. The entry of machines into the work place required the adoption of standardized parts: The push for "scientific" office management led to the adoption of the same sort of standards that regulated the size of screws, bolts, and other fasteners in the factory. Even the typewriter did not achieve acceptance until its keyboard was conventionalized in the famous QWERTY arrangement, itself a "scientifically" engineered standard.

Jefferson's dreams are now realized in the photocopier, computer, and laser printer for desktop publishing, and the digitization of documents in cyberspace. The evolution of office technologies between the eighteenth and twenty-first centuries—from the pantograph to the wireless Web—is the story of the dynamic interrelationship between invention and standards, freedom and connection, that characterized the nation's modern development.

### the telegraph: marching orders

It should be no surprise that the telegraph was developed in the United States. Rapid settlement across vast distances made the device ideal for America. The body politic of democracy and capitalism became a body electric. With the telegraph, for the first time in history, communication and trans-

portation were effectively separated. Until 1838 a written message had to be physically transported. The telegraph, invented by Samuel F.B. Morse, made information electrical for the first time. Morse code was the earliest form of software, demanding new kinds of clerks to code and decode it and new means of storage and transmission. Prefiguring the development of future office technology, the telegraph was a network system, dependent on accepted standards. Pioneered by an artist-tinkerer and implemented by financing from Congress, the telegraph established the pattern for the invention and production of successful office tools.[1]

The telegraph and the railroad functioned as sibling technologies, one directly following the other, together moving information and goods. Telegraph and rail helped realize the capacities of the American system of manufacture—the system of interchangeable parts pioneered by Eli Whitney (with Thomas Jefferson's sponsorship) and realized in the armories that made guns for the U.S. Army. The changes wrought by the railroad and telegraph came to a head during the Civil War, when both played major roles in troop deployment. The need to muster huge armies required expanding the parts system that would later extend to office machines. Firearms were not the only war machines to use the new parts system. To outfit the army, clothing and boot sizes were standardized in order to make use of sewing machines and other equipment.

Railroads and, later, businesses applied the wartime lessons of the efficiencies and economies gained from standards to post–Civil War enterprise. (These lessons also included adoption of the military's hierarchical organizational structures.) The paired technologies spread their networks across the landscape as the new American system of manufacturing grew, generating new military styles of organization as well as new types of office practice, storage, and employment. Bridging war and peace,

**Telautograph brochure showing transmitter and receiver,** 1893; Courtesy Warshaw Collection, Archives Center, National Museum of American History

The Gray National Telautograph Company of New York City developed this office machine, which instantaneously transmitted a copy of a document while it was being written. Electrical impulses sent over a wire moved the receiving pen in synch with the transmitting pen. The telautograph allowed easy communication between offices and their factories as well as between secretaries and bosses who could pass secret messages without a visitor's knowledge.

merging public and private enterprise, collapsing time and space, uniting the United States with the first electronic network, the telegraph was a device that anticipated almost all the changes in technology that later affected the office.

### the telephone: power talk

The advance from telegraph to telephone, from a digital to an analog device, was more than simply an evolution. It marked a shift to an entirely different form of information. Carrying voice as well as code over wires, the telephone undercut the hierarchies of military-style organizations and heightened individual power to command—or rebel.

Alexander Graham Bell first conceived the telephone in 1876 as a broadcast device for delivering concerts and speeches to a passive audience. It was

Theodore Vail, the power behind the rise of AT&T, who grasped the potential of the telephone and asserted the principle of universal phone service—the goal of putting a telephone in every home and office. Vail understood that the telephone was a network system, and that the law of networks is that each additional unit in the system increases the value of the whole exponentially.

The 1876 Centennial Exhibition in Philadelphia first showcased the telephone, but adoption was slow. As late as 1888, only sixty thousand telephones were installed. The real takeoff began in the 1890s as America's corporate and consumer cultures blossomed. From 1896 to 1899, the number of phones doubled, and from 1896 to 1906 it increased tenfold. By 1920 there were ten million telephones in the United States.

At first, as Roland Marchand pointed out, the telephone ruled in the office as a symbol of power. In advertisements the telephone on the large desk served as an icon of executive authority.[2] E.H. Harriman, the railroad magnate, was known for having telephones everywhere he went, in his many houses and even in his private rail car. One admiring observer of the time, Herbert Casson, commented that "what the brush is to the artist, what the chisel is to the sculptor, the telephone was to Harriman. He built his fortune on it."[3]

The telephone precipitated a major change in the face of American business. For the office, the telephone created a new relationship between the office and the outside world. In addition to the mailroom and visitor lobby or reception area, the switchboard, or PBX, served as the front face of the office.

**Advertisement, Bell Telephone System;** *Fortune*, June 1959

**Selectric Sequence Electronic Calculator,** 1948; Courtesy IBM Corporate Archives

"To answer your own phone" turned into a symbol of accessibility that no self-respecting executive could abide. One of the additional roles taken on by secretaries was to answer the phone and filter incoming calls, providing both a link to and a buffer between the outside world and the office.

## typewriter: machine tool

Like the American factory, the typewriter broke down the traditional hand labor of writing into discrete, repeatable mechanical pieces—its keys. The commercialization of the typewriter depended on the American system of interchangeable parts that had been pioneered for firearms. One of the first companies to successfully manufacture the machine was Remington, the gunmaker, looking for additional fields of enterprise after the Civil War.

Remington's first model went on the market in 1874 at a price of $125. It wasn't until more than a decade later that a manufacturer offered a typewriter whose typed line was visible to the user, or one with uppercase as well as lowercase letters. Although touch-typing came on the scene in the late 1880s, psychological barriers slowed the introduction of the typewriter into the office. Initially, documents produced on typewriters were confused with printed communications and were often considered impersonal and rude.

"Typewriter" was also the term given the operator of the machine—in many cases, a young woman. The machine and the woman arrived in offices together. Daniel Sutherland, in *The Expansion of Everyday Life, 1860–1876*, reported that women moved into the office during and after the Civil War.[4] Through the second half of the nineteenth century, the proportion of women clerical office workers increased steadily until, by 1920, they accounted for fully half of the work force. At first, the impetus was a shortage of male labor, but women soon proved themselves well-suited to operating the new office machinery. And, of course, women worked for less money than men. A male bookkeeper of the 1870s earned $1,800 a year, a woman only $500.

The typewriter and its operator quickly became inseparable: "Type girls" was a term in use by the 1870s. Mark Twain famously described one of the first demonstrations of the typewriter, in which a young woman repeatedly turned out high-speed copies of the poem beginning, "The boy stood on the burning deck." Twain found he did far less well himself and eventually hired an operator to turn out *Tom Sawyer*, the first typescript for a published book.

The typewriter, in effect, was a dictation machine, as oral information could be typed on a machine by a secretary. But the new secretary was no longer the copyist—a monklike scribe like Bartleby or Cratchit—but more like a multitasking industrial servant who answered the telephone, took dictation, typed, and filed.

The entrance of the typewriter into the office spurred other standards in office supplies and furniture. No less shrewd an observer than Le Corbusier, for example, noted how the typewriter propelled the adoption of the 8.5 x 11–inch sheet of paper as the standard business letter size, with corresponding carbon paper and envelopes to fit. The same dimensions ruled the size of file folders to hold documents and file cases to hold file folders. The desk, in turn, became conventionalized as filing drawers replaced the pigeonholed storage systems of the past, which kept papers rolled in scroll-like fashion and wrapped in the red tape that became the emblem of bureaucratic sloth. At the dawn of World War I, new "scientifically" designed and standardized desks, such as the Modern Efficiency Desk, replaced the private, hutchlike ones of the past. From this simple machine—the typewriter—an office landscape of efficiency and standardization developed.

**Elliot-Fisher Automatic Feed Machine brochure,** 1924; Courtesy Warshaw Collection, Archives Center, National Museum of American History,

This brochure for an automatic paper feeder links wartime efficiency and postwar business productivity. The feeder eliminated seven unnecessary steps in the production of office records. Working with a continuous paper roll, its operator could quickly enter information without the need to stop and reload order forms and carbon paper or to align margins.

The
Edison Business
Phonograph

The Dictator

The Stenographer

**Edison Business Phonograph brochure,** c. 1909; Courtesy Warshaw Collection, Archives Center, National Museum of American History

Edison conceived the phonograph as an office dictation machine, not an entertainment system.

Two ways to dictate...one cuts work in half

**DICTAPHONE** CORPORATION

**Advertisement, Dictaphone Corporation**
*Fortune,* June 1956

**IBM 224 Executary Dictation Machine,** 1965; Courtesy IBM Corporate Archives

### the dictation machine: words to go

The debut of the phonograph and its kin, almost simultaneous with the advent of the typewriter, offered the ability to record spoken words, then turn them into written text. Thomas Edison imagined the phonograph, invented in 1876, as a device for office dictation. Dictaphone, the company and trademark most closely associated with dictation equipment, had its roots in 1881, when Alexander Graham Bell developed an improved version of Edison's early phonograph. By 1888 the first commercial office dictation machine was in production. At that time it was called a "graphophone," derived from the term "gramophone." The device's wax cylinder, into which a needle inscribed grooves in response to speaking into a microphone, astonishingly remained in use as the recoding medium until 1947, when a rubberized belt was introduced to replace it. Later Dictaphones used plastic disks and, eventually, cassette tapes as recording media. These in turn have been succeeded by computer discs and chips, for wholly digital recording.

Mobile salespeople and caseworkers favored Dictaphones in order to quickly document case information on their return to the office, allowing more time outside in the field. In Billy Wilder's 1944 film *Double Indemnity,* an insurance salesman's Dictaphone took on a dramatic role as it became his confessional for a murder he helped commit.

In 1957 Dictaphone introduced its first portable unit: Weighing only two pounds, it freed the executive from his office. IBM followed in 1965 with its much-praised Model 224 unit. For the first time, important office technology became mobile.

**200,000 Wandering Boys,**
*Fortune*, February 1933; Illustrator:
F.V. Carpenter; Courtesy *Fortune*
© 1933 Time Inc. All rights reserved.

**Hollerith machine for keying punch cards,**
1915; Courtesy IBM Corporate Archives

## data processing: "punch photographs"

Like the telegraph, the development of data processing technology was sponsored by the federal government in an effort to create a system that would address the needs of a vast country. In this case, data processing originated as a means to take count of the nation's population, as mandated by the Constitution.

When the first American census took place in 1790, tabulating its data took nine months. The results of the 1880 census took seven years to compile. With the 1890 survey looming, Herman Hollerith, a former employee of the Census Bureau, built a tabulating machine that used punch cards to record and sort census information. He made the cards the same size as dollar bills so existing storage cabinets could be used. Hollerith's machines compiled the results of the 1890 census in six weeks, saving the Census Bureau $5 million in staff

costs. Without this technology, the census would have been impracticable at this date in the nation's history. This was the first of many instances in which the demands of government bureaucracy profoundly changed practices in private as well as public offices.

While Hollerith was familiar with the development of such cards for Jacquard looms, in use since the eighteenth century, he was initially inspired by a railroad conductor punching holes in a railroad ticket that offered means for recording information about passengers—sex, height, hair color, etc. This was called a punch photograph. Hollerith took the railroad ticket concept one step further, comparing the census itself to a huge photograph of the American population "full of life and vigor" made up of the punch photographs of individuals.[5]

Hollerith's cards had immediate applications for the railroads that had inspired him. They turned to the cards for tracking cargoes, employees, passengers, and other vital information. Other large corpo-

rations with information to record and manipulate followed. The New York Central Railroad hired Hollerith in 1896, the Marshall Field department store in 1903. Prudential Insurance and the Russian government were other clients. In 1911 Hollerith sold his tabulating machine company to the conglomerate that later became International Business Machines (IBM). The company developed Hollerith's idea, securing the future of data processing and launching the computer era. IBM assumed the leading role in the development of office technology that it occupied for the rest of the century.

The devices that handled, sorted, and compiled the data on cards became more sophisticated in the 1930s. What the census had done for the tabulating machine company, Social Security did for the new generation of IBM data-processing machines. The centerpiece of Franklin Delano Roosevelt's New Deal, Social Security, involved a level of bookkeeping complexity that only data-processing card systems

could handle. In 1936, the new Social Security Administration acquired some $1.5 million of data-processing equipment and millions of cards, all assembled in a huge facility in Baltimore.

Private corporations were also challenged by the data-keeping demands of the withholding tax, Workers Compensation, Social Security, and other government programs. Personnel and human resources departments grew in proportion to the increase in bureaucratic demands. Beginning in the 1940s, they too acquired data-processing equipment to handle increasingly complex functions of corporate administration.

### the pentagon, the mainframe computer, and systems thinking

Mustering human and material resources on an unprecedented scale was the task of the Pentagon, planned in 1941 as the world's largest office building—even before Pearl Harbor. Taking its shape from a traditional five-sided fortification, the building became a symbol of the new blending of government, military, science, and academia.

Among the Pentagon's contributions to postwar business culture was the creation of the digital computer, which was originally conceived to calculate complex artillery trajectories and then was quickly applied to code-breaking and other tasks. After World War II, the computer was adopted by private enterprise. Administering such vast military projects, argued Thomas P. Hughes in his study of massive modern projects, *Rescuing Prometheus*, led to the rise of systems thinking, analysis, and planning that grew in symbiosis with computers. Systems thinking, which analyzed the function and flow of information as a whole, dominated the 1950s economic landscape and the Cold War, reshaping the office in the process.[6]

"The system is the solution," AT&T's famous postwar slogan, was the mantra of all corporate America in the 1950s and 1960s. From the sort of big business Alfred Chandler described in his book *The Visible Hand* to the contractors, research labs, and think tanks of the military-industrial-academic complex, the systems ethos built on and ultimately superceded Taylorite visions of the office.

The icon of systems thinking was the mainframe computer, a force at once marvelous and intimidating. The new computers figured in the office landscape like huge pieces of industrial machinery requiring constant care and feeding (and often requiring their own sequestered offices). An established trope in popular culture by the early 1950s, with blinking lights flashing patterns meaningless to humans, the mainframe inspired visions of dystopia as much as utopia. More lightly treated, the mainframe was contrasted with the human element in such films as *Desk Set* (1957) with Katharine Hepburn and Spencer Tracy, which concluded with the marriage of Hepburn's hands-on methods of information retrieval and Tracy's computer technologies.

Offices for business systems housed large numbers of people laboring on standardized modules of work. Some aerospace firms actually calculated the number of engineers needed for a particular project by the acre. The private office increasingly became a rare refuge for top executives. More typical was the large office plain dotted with identical desks. If the early upright desk with its pigeonholes resembled a kind of cottage, then the low desks that were state-of-the-art for the postwar Fortune 500 suggested suburban landscapes—ranch houses laid out across a vast residential development.

These office landscapes and the culture they embodied soon were as critically treated as suburbia itself in such books as William H. Whyte's *The Organization Man*. John Kenneth Galbraith's attack in *The Affluent Society* (1958) sharpened in *The New*

*Industrial State* (1967), which depicted a management class whose goal had become its own perpetuation. The punch card was derided as a symbol of inhumanity and impersonality. "I am a human being," read a popular T-shirt slogan of the late 1960s, parodying the legend printed on each IBM card: "Do not fold, spindle, or mutilate."

But new technologies that would radically change the equipment on the office desktop in the 1980s were already taking shape in Pentagon projects of the 1950s and 1960s. As a byproduct of its defense systems, military technology unwittingly provided the means for more personal alternatives to centralized systems. The needs of air defense to combine a vast network of distant radar stations led to the networking of computers. At the same time, the requirement to display targets visually spurred innovations in monitors and control devices for computers. Such projects as the SAGE air defense system, which visually presented centralized information

about the location of dozens of airplanes tracked by distant radar stations, prefigured today's office networks and the rising power of data processing in corporate America.

These network technologies would ultimately supercede the mainframe model. The Advanced Research Projects Agency (ARPA), established in the wake of the Soviet Union's 1957 launch of Sputnik, and the Pentagon's Information Processing Techniques Office (IPTO) of the 1960s became seedbeds for many vital computer technologies, from time sharing to packet switching. These new technologies made possible large-scale networks of geographically separated computers, as well as user interfaces deployed by the mouse. (The mouse was developed in 1969 by Douglas Engelbart under an ARPA grant, as the x-y pointing device.) Also of tremendous consequence to today's contemporary office technology was ARPA's development of an email system: The first email was sent in 1972

through the ARPAnet. In the wings were devices such as the personal computer that provided successors to the telegraph network and the typewriter.

## electric typewriters: a factory of words

Solo inventor James Smathers had pioneered the electric typewriter before World War I, but through the 1920s sales amounted to only a few thousand units. Smathers's technology, refined and improved, was put into production by the Electromatic Corporation in the 1920s. There, it attracted the attention of IBM, which bought out Electromatic in 1933. Launched in the face of the Depression, the first electric typewriter with the IBM nameplate came on the market in 1935. To promote the machine, IBM hired champion typist Margaret Hamma to give demonstrations, during which she reached speeds of up to 150 words per minute while balancing cups of water on the backs of her hands. This illustrated

**IBM 701 Mainframe Computer,** 1952;
Courtesy IBM Corporate Archives

"Golf ball" element for
**IBM Selectric typewriter,** 1961;
Courtesy IBM Corporate Archives

how little effort the typewriter took and how much effort it saved the user. The advantages of the electric typewriter, however, lay as much in producing multiple copies as in achieving sheer speed. By 1975, reported the *New York Times,* approximately 75 percent of the million typewriters sold were electric.[7]

Electric typewriters were essentially mechanical ones assisted by motors. But a radically different kind of typewriter arrived when IBM launched the Selectric model in 1961. Letters were mounted on a golf ball–type unit, rather than the individual mechanical keys of the past. These units, made in various fonts, were interchangeable, allowing one machine to produce multiple typefaces. This change was symbolized in the Selectric's form, which represented a new vision for the design of technology. The outer shell of the machine was designed by Eliot Noyes to reflect the theme of the golf ball print unit, but its geometry was softened into a more natural shape inspired by the ideals of biomorphism. Noyes

wanted the Selectric to recall a Noguchi sculpture, creating a soothing presence in the otherwise rigid geometry of the contemporary office.

As a platform from which typing could evolve toward the manipulation of text, the electric typewriter represented a transition toward the personal computer and printer. The new generation of typewriters that began to appear in the 1960s allowed for the storage of text. At first these memories were mechanical, as in the early Selectrics that stayed a keystroke or two behind in order to allow for instant corrections. Later, they used electronic chips and electronic media such as tape to store frequently used, or "boilerplate," text such as standard contracts or letters.

A 1974 *New York Times* article cited growth in the typewriter market as the coming of age of "word processing."[8] Inspired by "data processing," the term was coined by electric typewriter salespeople and defined by IBM as "the transition of a written, verbal

**IBM Selectric typewriter,** 1961;
Designer: Eliot Noyes;
Courtesy IBM Corporate Archives

**Skyscrapers: Pyramids in Steel & Stock,**
*Fortune,* August 1930; Illustrator: Walter Buehr; Courtesy *Fortune* © 1930 Time Inc. All rights reserved.

113

or recorded idea to final typewritten or printed form."[9] Executives who watched the average time and labor costs of a business letter rise during the 1960s viewed word processing as a way to lower it. In word processing, recorded dictation was sent to a typing pool. This new system, according to John McDonald, a vice president of marketing for Sperry Rand's office products division, was "an attempt to handle words the way a computer handles numbers—breaking down secretarial labor into distinct components."[10] An IBM executive proclaimed that "the efficiency techniques that were shown successful for factory and accounting departments are now being proven equally useful in offices."[11] Like data processing, word processing centralized an office process—specifically the dictation/typing process—and broke it down into components. Like the factory assembly line, it dedicated specific equipment and workers to each part of the process in order to lower costs. The dedicated word processing computer enjoyed only a short life, however, before the more versatile personal computer arrived.

## the personal computer

The step from the word processor to the multipurpose personal computer (PC) was a natural one. Developed by hobbyists in the mid-1970s, the personal computer was recast as a business machine with the introduction of IBM's first model, the IBM Personal Computer, in 1981. Significantly, IBM's PC was presented in a memorable ad campaign based on images from *Modern Times*, Charlie Chaplin's landmark 1936 film, which represented a famous attack on the inhumanity of Taylor-style manufacturing. The Tramp's personal computer apparently enabled him to do without a desk at all. The advertisements showed him free to roam about, his computer sitting atop a Saarinen-style tulip side table of the sort found in reception areas. Beside the computer on the table

was a single rose in a vase—a distant but distinct echo of "flower power."

Skating happily about, the Little Tramp and his personal computer suggested liberation from the Taylorite vision by fulfilling it. In images taken from *Modern Times* in which Chaplin rollerskates through a department store, IBM's ads showed the computer as a tool to manage factory and warehouse—putting the big gears in individual and human control. It was a happy vision of computer potential that contrasted with the oppressions of the factory system and the mainframe computer.

The personal computer's ambition to replace the conventional desk was manifested in the 1984 advent of the Apple Macintosh computer. Using a "desktop metaphor," Macintosh projected the computer screen as a virtual desktop, with programs designated by icons pulled from storage—not in drawers but in computer memory. To organize software these icons, or small ideograms, presented images of corresponding physical devices—a text program was represented by a pen or quill, an address file by a Rolodex, etc. The desk had migrated inside the works of the computer.[12]

In spite of the intent to replace the desk with the virtual desktop, the PC's attached peripherals, from printers to storage disks and scanners, soon took over the actual desktop, elbowing aside earlier devices. Furniture makers responded by designing desks with sliding keyboard trays and secondary computer stands, thereby reincarnating the typing table in a new form.

The computer would ultimately triumph in the office via "desktop publishing," which required that computers be attached to high-quality printers. These printers were an outgrowth of the photocopier, the device that almost as much as the computer did away with the old manual work of the copyist.

Photocopying has long been a business ideal. Just as Western Union dismissed the importance of

**IBM personal computer,**
1981; Courtesy IBM
Corporate Archives

**Xerox 914 copier,** 1960;
© 1960 Xerox Corporation.
All rights reserved.

the telephone, IBM turned down the photocopier originally developed in the 1930s by Chester "Chet" Carlson, the classic solo inventor who carried out his first experiments in an apartment above a Queens, New York, beauty parlor. It took a speculative investment by the Batelle Foundation after World War II to create the Xerox Corporation around Carlson's invention. Although the company was profitable by the mid-1950s, Xerox sales zoomed with its introduction of the Model 914 in 1960. Soon familiar in every office as a gathering spot for workers, the photocopier represented another implicit message: Unchecked reproduction of documents actually undermines central control. The tight restrictions on copying machines in totalitarian societies (consider the Xerox distribution of underground literature in Russia) and the Daniel Ellsburg Pentagon Papers case suggested the power of copying machines to let the individual escape a central structure. (Significantly, it was Xerox's advanced development facility in Palo Alto, California, that served as the incubator for the personal computer—the ultimate symbol of liberating technology.)

Xerox executives did not want to miss out on the "next Xerox." They shrewdly understood that the company was in the "office document" business and not just the photocopier business. In response, they set up a large and aggressive office for research and development in Palo Alto that would eventually help integrate computer, copier, and telephone transmission. (The transmission of images over wires has a long history in the equipment used by news-wire services to disseminate photographs in crude efforts to distribute newspapers by telephone to home and office.) Combining the copier and the telephone, Xerox's Telecopier of 1976 is generally cited as the first commercially available facsimile machine. But it was not until the early 1980s, when international agencies standardized fax transmission protocols, that the technology really took off. By that time

Japanese companies such as Canon and Toshiba had succeeded in producing lower-cost machines. By the summer of 1986, facsimile transmission became cheaper than international telex. The number of fax machines nearly doubled between 1987 and 1988. The November 1988 cover story in *New York* magazine heralded the fax's fashionability by noting that the word "fax" had become a verb as well as a noun.[13]

Capable of transmitting images as well as words and numbers, the fax became an essential business technology with the unprecedented capacity to communicate documents immediately. It was of particular benefit to companies whose engineering and design staffs might be located in Europe or the United States and their factories in Asia. Few office technologies had ever become so essential so quickly. It became another node that connected the office to the outside world, while centralizing its own social relations, as the switchboard and the photocopier had.

Almost as quickly, however, fax machines became components of personal computers, decentralized and available at every desk.

### *from desktop to laptop*

The personal computer challenged the data-processing departments that had become powerful forces in many companies. The PC undermined the degree of control a company could exercise over its machines and, consequently, its employees. Beginning with portable computers such as the Osborne and Kaypro, the computer began to leave the office. Adam Osborne, who created the first portable personal computer in 1981, promised "to drive secretaries out of every office in America."[14] But secretaries, many of whom were now called "executive assistants," were marks of prestige too important for executives to give up overnight. And many executives and managers lacked typing skills,

**IBM ThinkPad 380D,** c. 1997
Courtesy IBM Corporate Archives

**Advertising image (detail), for
Librex laptop computers,** early
1990s; Courtesy Phil Patton

not to mention the willingness to learn new technologies, even if those technologies would make them more efficient. As the PC became an obligatory symbol of being up-to-date, it sat little-used behind an executive's traditional desk.

The portable computer was different. The first important laptop was the Grid Compass (1982), which helped establish the form of the traveling computer. As the large mahogany desk had previously signaled executive power, the thin black laptop came to identify corporate energy in the 1980s. The names of such products as IBM's ThinkPad and Apple's Powerbook suggested brainpower and strength. By the 1980s the shape was clear: a crisp black rectangle (inspired in part by camera and firearm design), a power icon that succeeded the mainframe and the desktop PC as a totem of office technology. By the 1990s, a decade that celebrated the entrepreneur, a prestigious office was not a large suite with a vast wooden desk and high-back chair.

Instead, the new CEO's office was a laptop and an Adirondack chair in the wilderness—at least according to computer company advertising.

### *personal digital assistants: from virtual desktop to virtual office*

In the 1980s, admiration for Japanese economic success helped reshape American industry and the American office. Growing out of the rethinking of Taylorite manufacturing, ideals of "lean" or "just-in-time" manufacturing fascinated Americans in the 1980s. Inspired by a Japan that had carried Taylor-style scientific management to a higher level of refinement and humanity, Americans placed new emphasis on teamwork in the office. In addition, planning and "knowledge work"—or what economist Robert B. Reich, former secretary of labor under Bill Clinton, called "symbol manipulation"—became a new focus for office planners.[15]

One result was the abandonment of the traditional office entirely. Just-in-time production led to just-in-time office work. Employees might work at home, by telecommuting, or drop in at the office according to the needs of a project rather than a punch clock. The number of workers at home doubled to 25 million between 1983 and 1993. Less high-minded motives for embracing telecommuting or the virtual office were pressures to reduce the cost of office space and the need to attract skilled employees, who had become scarce, with amenities such as flexible working conditions.

Such efforts were abetted by the new generation of computer devices known as personal digital assistants (PDAs), which began to appear in the late 1980s and early 1990s and soon became widespread. These portable devices work without keyboards, using a stylus and handwriting recognition. But many of them have retained the desktop metaphor. From Apple's Newton, publicized under

**SONY Magic Link personal communicator digital assistant,** 1994; Courtesy SONY

**Advertisement, Stromberg-Carlson Company;** *Fortune,* June 1956

Early pagers such as the Pagemaster were marketed primarily to executives, in contrast to the democracy of such devices today.

the slogan "Put your office in the palm of your hand," to the Palmpilot, the prevailing metaphor is a desk that fits in a coat pocket.

One of the prophets of the virtual office was Michael Bell, director of corporate real estate for Dun & Bradstreet. The term "office," he asserted in the early 1990s, should be considered a verb and not a noun.[16] The office should now be rethought as a place for inspiration and socializing. In part, the change to the mobile office came in reaction to changes in the economy, especially the rising importance of knowledge-based industries. The number of temporary employees in American offices was also increasing. Soon the nation's largest employer was not General Motors or Procter & Gamble but Manpower, a temporary office help agency. The transition in office function accelerated with the increasing importance of services over goods in the economy.

Perhaps the best known virtual office experiment was conducted by the advertising agency Chiat/Day, in a Venice, California, building designed by Frank Gehry. Instead of a traditional office and desk, or a workstation, workers could seek inspiration and fellowship in spaces variously called the student union, club room, romper room, and conference womb. Tilt-a-Whirl conference spaces were created in cars borrowed from old amusement park rides.[17]

Chiat/Day soon opened a similar virtual office designed by Gaetano Pesce in New York, but both offices were abandoned after only a year. Chiat/Day's experiment was considered less than a rousing success, although it is hard to determine whether difficulties inherent in the virtual office concept were to blame. Practical or not, the dream of the virtual office and the freedom it promises continues to hold a strong attraction. Some office experts such as Michael Bell of Dun & Bradstreet or management gurus like Tom Peters suggest that the office is only necessary as a link to files and file

servers. However portable new devices are, they must still retain access to common equipment.

The challenge of linking personal computers to each other and to common servers has occupied engineers for a long time, as they have developed local area networks with such technologies as Ethernet. Electrical cords and data cabling were always a problem in that they created tangled messes and are hard to move. More and more wires multiplied the difficulties. In the 1970s, some office interior designers adopted the strategy of restaurants and retail establishments by leaving wires, pipes, and HVAC vents exposed.[18] By the 1990s the wires that linked computers to each other and to the Internet joined plumbing and mechanical devices in this open, informal display. In high-tech companies, the informality sometimes extended to desks, laden with computer equipment, made of doors on top of sawhorses.

This ad hoc style characterized the offices of the Internet company Razorfish, which moved into the space vacated by Chiat/Day in Los Angeles in 1998. Semiscreened computer stations, linked to the company Intranet and the Internet beyond, are joined by visible wires. At the New York Razorfish office, the visual focus of the space is the Internet server and router system: The computer linking the office to the wired world beyond is proudly displayed behind glass, as mainframes had been forty years before. Beside the router room stands a display of obsolete portable computing equipment—like the booty of captured nations hauled before a Roman imperial arch of triumph. If portability and mobility are a challenge to the office based on individuality, a countervailing desire for connection and the power it brought are displayed here. Increasingly, wireless devices such as cell phones and PDAs seem to be merging into a single unit—a new version of the portable desk Jefferson designed to carry from Monticello to Philadelphia and Washington. A key phrase at the turn of the twenty-first century that looks to a convergence of telephone and computer is "wireless Web," an image suggesting the continuing tension between independence and mobility, on the one hand, and centralization and connection, on the other.

This age-old American tension has been recast in the vision of the office as a place to be escaped from but never out of touch with, a locale for innovation but also for shared standards. This new office is the latest proof that technology, which has always come to the office as a new means for individual expression, ends up as confirmation of the need for common ground.

1. Tom Standage, *The Victorian Internet: The Remarkable Story of the Telegraph and the Nineteenth Century's On-Line Pioneers* (New York: Walker, 1998).

2. Roland Marchand, *Advertising the American Dream: Making Way for Modernity, 1920–1940* (Berkeley: University of California Press, 1985), 239–42.

3. Herbert N. Casson, *History of the Telephone* (1910; reprint, Freeport, N.Y.: Books for Libraries Press, 1971), 159.

4. Daniel E. Sutherland, *The Expansion of Everyday Life, 1860–1876* (New York: Harper & Row, 1989), 202–04.

5. Herman Hollerith quoted by Geoffrey D. Austrian, *Herman Hollerith: Forgotten Giant of Information Processing* (New York: Columbia University Press, 1982), 88–89.

6. Thomas P. Hughes, *Rescuing Prometheus* (New York: Pantheon, 1998), 141–95.

7. William D. Smith, "Electric Typewriter Sales Are Bolstered by Efficiency, *New York Times* (December 16, 1974).

8. Ibid.

9. Ibid.

10. John McDonald, quoted in Smith, "Electric Typewriter Sales."

11. Background Paper on IBM Electric Typewriters, IBM Press Relations, Armonk, New York, c. 1980.

12. The virtual desktop was originally developed at Xerox's Palo Alto Research Center, which first applied it in the ALTO computer. Xerox researchers Alan Kay went to Apple and Charles Simonyi to Microsoft, where he helped create Windows, Microsoft's version of the graphical user interface.

13. David Blum, "Fax Mania," *New York* (November 21, 1988), 40–44.

14. Adam Osborne, Author interview, 1982.

15. Robert B. Reich, *The Work of Nations: Preparing Ourselves for 21st-century Capitalism* (New York: Alfred A. Knopf, 1991).

16. Michael Bell, "The Virtual Office: Alternative Work Styles and Places in a Knowledge-based, Global Economy," unpublished 1993 lecture.

17. Phil Patton, "The Virtual Office Becomes Reality," *New York Times* (October 28, 1993), Section C, 1 and 6.

18. Joan Kron and Suzanne Slesin, *High Tech: The Industrial Style and Sourcebook for the Home* (New York: Clarkson Potter, 1978).

**AT&T Travel Guide concept with global positioning system,** 1999; Designer: frogdesign Courtesy frogdesign

While exploring or just roaming, the Travel Guide will be able to provide instant information via the Internet and a wireless network.

**AT&T Watchphone concept,** 1999; Designer: frogdesign; Courtesy frogdesign

The Watchphone features an ingenious tool–the dialing device detaches from the watch to become an earpiece.

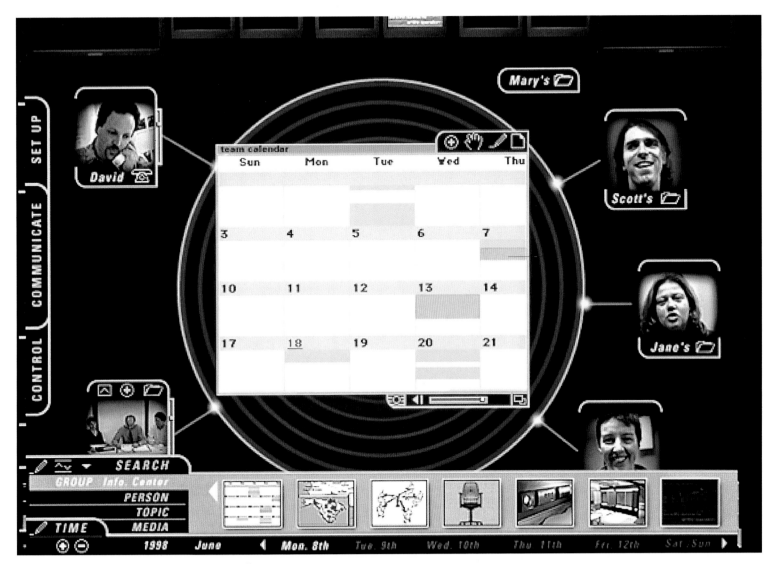

**Steelcase Globe Project Conferencing System,** 1999; Designer: Steelcase and IDEO; Courtesy IDEO

The Globe Project allows office workers—both in the room and connected remotely—to display, store, and retrieve electronic documents and data.
The concept humanizes the computer screen and creates a sense of shared office space.

# *knowing glances*

Intercoms, telephones, fax, and email are only a few of the ways that office workers communicate with each other. Business culture, as "Office Intrigues" underscores, is a complex and complicated animal. These images record the knowing glances that transmit unspoken messages about power, hierarchy, and sexual politics. Most graphically represented in films, television programs, and magazine articles about American daily life, these looks pass every day between men and women, boss and underling, sexual predator and prey.
—D.A., C.B.B.

*Window Washer*, 1960; Illustrator: Norman Rockwell Cover art for the *Saturday Evening Post*, September 17, 1960; © Curtis Publishing Company

*Office at Night* (facing page), 1940; Artist: Edward Hopper; Courtesy Walker Art Center, Minneapolis, Minnesota; Gift of the T.B. Walker Foundation, Gilbert M. Walker Fund, 1948

**Fred MacMurray and Edie Adams in *The Apartment*,** 1960; Courtesy Everett Collection and Metro-Goldwyn-Mayer Inc./ United Artists.

The disapproving glance of Adams's executive secretary indicates who really has the upper hand in this work relationship. Adams eventually eavesdrops on MacMurray's private telephone conversations, blowing the whistle on her boss's extramarital affairs.

MR. BROCKTON

*Office Love,* 1978;
Photographer: Helmut Newton;
© Helmut Newton TDR

**Michael Douglas and Demi Moore in *Disclosure*,** 1994;
*Disclosure* © 1994 Warner Brothers, a division of Time Warner Entertainment Company, L.P. All rights reserved.

No one seems to mind working late in this Seattle office. Douglas ends up suing his boss, played by Moore, in this role-reversing twist on sexual harassment.

Ed Asner and Mary Tyler Moore
in *The Mary Tyler Moore Show*,
1970–77; Courtesy CBS Photo
Archive

## corporate officers who are women

8.7%   10.0%   10.6%   11.2%   11.9%

'95 '96 '97 '98 '99

NUMBERS IN THOUSANDS      MEN      WOMEN

## men vs. women in the workforce

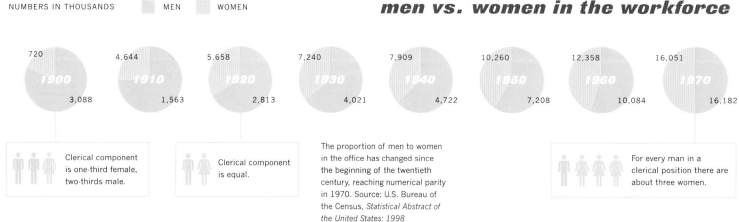

| | | | | | | | |
|---|---|---|---|---|---|---|---|
| 720 | 4,644 | 5,658 | 7,240 | 7,909 | 10,260 | 12,358 | 16,051 |
| 1900 | 1910 | 1920 | 1930 | 1940 | 1950 | 1960 | 1970 |
| 3,088 | 1,563 | 2,813 | 4,021 | 4,722 | 7,208 | 10,084 | 16,182 |

Clerical component
is one-third female,
two-thirds male.

Clerical component
is equal.

The proportion of men to women
in the office has changed since
the beginning of the twentieth
century, reaching numerical parity
in 1970. Source: U.S. Bureau of
the Census, *Statistical Abstract of
the United States: 1998*

For every man in a
clerical position there are
about three women.

Unisex bathroom in *Ally McBeal*,
1998; © Twentieth Century Fox
Film Corporation. All rights
reserved.

## executive men vs. women

In the office, women and
men may be equal numerically,
but women still lag far behind
their co-workers in rank.
Source: Catalyst

### chief executive

TOTAL OFFICERS 506    NUMBER OF WOMEN 4

### chairman

TOTAL OFFICERS 61    NUMBER OF WOMEN 0

### vice chairman

TOTAL OFFICERS 193    NUMBER OF WOMEN 6

### president

TOTAL OFFICERS 206    NUMBER OF WOMEN 4

### chief operating officer

TOTAL OFFICERS 39    NUMBER OF WOMEN 0

### senior executive vice president

TOTAL OFFICERS 42    NUMBER OF WOMEN 4

### executive vice president

TOTAL OFFICERS 1,202    NUMBER OF WOMEN 98

**America Online's Creative Center 1,** 1999; Dulles, Virginia
Architect: Ai; Photographer:
© Jeff Goldberg/Esto

Ai transformed this former aerospace warehouse into a state-of-the-art office building in only eight months. Creative Center 1 is part of AOL's headquarter campus of nearly 120 acres outside Washington, D.C. (An interior view of another AOL building on the same campus, its corporate headquarters, is illustrated on the adjacent page.)

# office intrigues
## the interior life of corporate culture

**Thomas Hine**

**Robert W. Pittman, President of America Online, in his office,** 1998; Photographer: © Peter Murphy; Courtesy Corbis Outline

"A Bridge Builder for Corporate Culture" read the main headline on the *New York Times* Business Day section of January 12, 2000. The story, a follow-up to the acquisition of Time Warner by America Online, shows a man seated in an ergonomic chair next to a slablike table in an inexpensively carpeted room whose wall of windows seems to overlook a muddy construction site. The chair is more a secretarial model than a presidential one, but it turns out that the man in the picture is Robert W. Pittman, president of America Online and a former employee of Warner Communications.

Two other photographs illustrate the story. One shows a transparent and seemingly empty exurban building—America Online's headquarters, adjacent to Dulles Airport outside Washington, D.C. The other is a view of what the caption calls "Time Warner's Manhattan monolith," a limestone-clad slab in Rockefeller Center.

The contrast between the new-media culture—transparent, open, cheap—and the old-media culture—stone-faced, closed, opulent—couldn't be more apparent. It also seems to bear out what has become conventional wisdom at the turn of the twenty-first century: The business with the cheapest office space will prevail. In contrast to the 1980s, when companies sought to identify themselves with marble veneer lobbies and rosewood boardrooms, today's successful corporate predator seeks speculative office space, furnished as anonymously as possible.

Even as branding becomes more important, the institutions that grew up around the brands and gave them value, or at least continuity, are being stripped away in the name of efficiency. A well-developed corporate culture was once defined as an asset. Now it is often considered a liability. The remnants of the cultures of merged and acquired companies bear much of the blame when grand schemes do not work. And because success is often defined by cost savings—getting rid of employees—stockholders view culture as resistance to profitability.

This is, then, a peculiar time to be writing of the relationship between design and corporate culture. From the point of view of investors, the best corporate culture appears to be none at all—or, at most, a nomadic one that travels light and lives off its plunder.

In the case of the America Online-Time Warner union, it was announced that the merged company will have its headquarters in a new tower to be built on New York's Columbus Circle. It looks as if the barbarians might end up turning themselves into Romans after all. AOL stock plummeted accordingly.[1]

Despite what the *New York Times* spread implied, corporate culture is not something you can take a picture of. It is shaped not by furniture or a building's exterior but by the people who constitute the company. Here is another way of looking at corporate culture:

> In the office in which I work there are five people of whom I am afraid. Each of these five people is afraid of four people (excluding overlaps) for a total of twenty, and each of these twenty people is afraid of six people, making a total of one hundred and twenty people who are feared by at least one other person. . . . Nobody is sure anymore who really runs the company (not even the people who are credited with running it), but the company does run.

—Joseph Heller, *Something Happened* (1974)[2]

Heller's charting of the patterns of fear in an office has some of the quality of anthropological research about the relationships in, for example, a New Guinea village. This reminds us that corporate culture is a concept taken from anthropology. Edgar H. Schein, professor emeritus of management at Massachusetts Institute of Technology defines corporate culture as "learned, shared tacit assumptions on which people base their daily behavior.

"Culture is so stable and so difficult to change," Schein writes, "because it represents the accumulated learning of a group—the ways of thinking, feeling and perceiving the world that have made the group successful." He adds, "The important parts of a culture are essentially invisible. Culture at this deep level can be thought of as shared mental models that the members of an organization hold and take for granted. They cannot readily tell you what their culture is, any more than fish, if they could talk, could tell you what water is."[3] You can't invent a new corporate culture every Monday morning and, if you try, your efforts will simply become noise that those within the culture tune out. Employees know that hotshots come and go and that nominally revolutionary ideas come along from time to time, but these burn themselves out. The way things are done, the ways in which status is defined, the ways people relate to one another, the kinds of actions that lead to job promotions—barring merger, acquisition, or catastrophe—change slowly.

As Schein says, culture is learned, but it is rarely taught. One absorbs culture by looking around, seeing what happens, and hearing what people say. If participants in a culture view that culture as arbitrary, as a matter of choice that could well be different, it's not really functioning as a culture. If you're in it, culture tends to be invisible. It is simply an aspect of reality.

Thus, while some aspects of cultures within a corporation are expressed in its physical environment, you can't know anything definitive about the culture simply by looking once at the office. And while hundreds of companies include a statement on their Web sites about corporate culture—usually

**Skeleton in Cubicle,** 1997;
Illustrator: Tom Cheney;
*New Yorker*, October 20, 1997;
© The New Yorker
Collection, cartoonbank.com.
All rights reserved.

**Dilbert® cartoon,** September 15, 1996; Cartoonist: Scott Adams; Color version from *Journey to Cubeville* by Scott Adams. © 1998 United Feature Syndicate. Published by Andrews McMeel Publishing, Kansas City, Missouri.

in the portion dedicated to recruiting employees—you can't really reduce it to a few words. Most attempts to express and elucidate a corporate culture turn out to be either exercises in self-deception or attempts to manipulate and change the culture. Corporate culture may be entwined with the mission and values of the company, but it is far more complex than a mission statement. Culture contributes to the public perception of a company, but it is not synonymous with corporate image-making. Indeed, it is almost the opposite. Public relations is about expressing a clear, carefully considered message. Corporate culture contains many messages, some may directly contradict the publicists' image, and nearly all go unexpressed.

It seems logical that the setting in which corporate culture plays out must have some substantial role in shaping it, much as a desert setting or a rain forest creates limits and expectations for people living there. This assumption is frequently alluded to, if not explored, in the pages of design magazines. Descriptions of office design projects say, for example, that the designer was asked by the client "to enhance corporate culture," or a client's representative will say that the "energy and vitality of our corporate culture" went unexpressed in the firm's previous office.[4] Recently, vital corporate culture has been identified primarily with providing places for the informal exchange of ideas and for collaboration and team building. Openness, whimsy, and the reuse of lofts, warehouses, or old bowling alleys are seen as markers of a culture of creativity. The rabbit-warren offices depicted in the comic strip *Dilbert* are seldom seen in design magazines. If they are, the writers, designers, and clients surely see them in a different way than do the cubicle dwellers trapped within them.

Different sorts of businesses create different sorts of interiors. Law firms, for example, are associated with numerous private offices and highly tra-

ditional decorative styles. Banks might be equally traditional in their public areas, but there is often little or no visual privacy although very private matters are discussed. The difference can be explained, in part, by the nature of the business being conducted. Lawyers are advocates for individuals; they need to reassure clients that nothing they say will leave the room. Bankers, however, represent a community of savers, borrowers, and investors, and when you are transacting business with them, the eyes of this community are upon you.

Financial trading floors are arranged bullpen-style—entirely open and noisy, with the hygiene standards of a pigsty. Like old-fashioned newspaper offices, which they resemble, their very hubbub creates a zone of privacy for the many individuals who are pursuing their narrow specialties, yet the space also communicates a sense of the collective endeavor and the urgency of their tasks.[5] Offices for advertising agencies and entertainment companies have almost an obligation to be unconventional because clients come to them for offbeat, creative thinking.

During the 1980s and early 1990s, many companies created opulent headquarters that contained only relatively high-level staff, while the "back office" was housed in sprawling, spartan workspaces in the suburbs, or another state or country. These separate installations had cultures of their own.

The very location of an office might help create its corporate culture. That's what William H. Whyte argued in his 1988 book *City: Rediscovering the Center.* He studied the thirty-eight major companies that had moved their headquarters from Manhattan between 1976 and 1987 and compared them with the thirty-six that had stayed. His first finding was that nearly half the companies that moved had lost their identity during that period, either by merger or failure. Then he compared the stock price of those that had gone, which rose, on average, 107

**Lobby of the Republic Bank
of Houston (RepublicBank Center),**
1983; Houston, Texas; Architect:
Johnson Burgee Architects;
Interior designer: Gensler;
Photographer: Chas McGrath;
Courtesy Gensler

## downtown vs. suburbs

**legal service companies**  82% CENTRAL BUSINESS DISTRICTS

**insurance companies**  50% CENTRAL BUSINESS DISTRICTS
50% SUBURBAN LOCATIONS

**high-tech companies**  22% CENTRAL BUSINESS DISTRICTS
34% OFFICE PARKS
44% SUBURBAN LOCATIONS

ONE SYMBOL = TEN PERCENT

In today's economy, different types
of businesses want different locations.
Source: "What Office Tenants Want"
(1999), Building Owners and
Managers Association and Urban
Land Institute

**Associate-level office at the law firm of Davis Polk & Wardwell,**
1988; New York, New York;
Interior designer: Gensler;
Photographer: Nick Merrick;
Courtesy Gensler

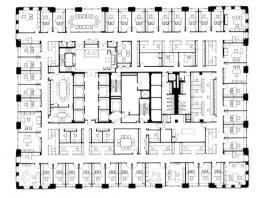

**Floor plan of the law firm of Davis Polk & Wardwell,** 1992;
New York, New York;
Courtesy Gensler

percent, with that of those that had stayed, which rose 277 percent. His conclusion was that people are inspired and energized by an intense setting filled with busy people, and that isolating a company imposes a cost.[6] In other words, Whyte argued, corporate culture benefits from exposure to the culture at large.

In casting his argument in terms of New York, however, Whyte was making a case for traditional urban places, such as busy streets and plazas, and urban institutions, such as theaters, museums, and restaurants. In the years since, New York has grown ever more specialized as a generator and showcase for what is now called "content," such as books, magazines, advertising, television, and online information, and as a center for a financial services industry that is, nevertheless, becoming steadily decentralized. Decisions about the companies and technologies reshaping this changing world are increasingly made elsewhere. California's Silicon Valley, arguably the center of the wired economy, works much like a great city. It has a large pool of highly specialized talent and well-informed, venturesome sources of capital. It does not, however, look much like a city, nor does it offer visitors any way to partake in its energy and excitement. By all accounts, though, companies doing business there are not obsessed with their own corporate cultures, for they live in a place that forces them to be aware of a wider world—which is what Whyte was really talking about.

Given that corporate culture seems to be so much on the minds of designers and their clients, one might think that those who study the subject would be interested in design—but one would be wrong. The literature on organizational theory is almost entirely devoid of studies of the impact of buildings and their furnishings and configuration on corporate culture, or vice versa. One such work, a collection of essays edited by Pasquale Gagliardi, began with this statement: "The study of physical setting as a source of sensory, emotional and symbolic experiences has had an altogether marginal role in organization theory."[7] Gagliardi went on to prove this point by citing scholars who have found the design of offices and their artifacts insignificant or uninteresting. The physical surroundings of work are viewed almost entirely as an area where things can go wrong—workplace accidents, repetitive-stress injuries, sick building syndrome—rather than as places that support or embody corporate culture.

One could more easily understand this neglect of office design if organizational theorists actually behaved like anthropologists and attempted to consider and analyze cultures on their own terms. The constituency for information about corporate culture, however, is primarily top managers who wonder why their companies won't do what they want them to do. They seek advice about how to use the culture to get their way.

An anthropologist and one of the current leaders in this field is Karen Stephenson, a professor at the University of California at Los Angeles Anderson Graduate School of Management, who has developed a software program to help managers understand and intervene in their cultures. She views corporate culture in terms of the dissemination and analysis of information. Stephenson characterizes key employees as "hubs," people who are centers of information within a group; "gatekeepers," people who facilitate or block communication among groups; and "pulse-takers," close observers whose analyses are heeded by others. She advises executives to make use of these nonhierarchical and reliable communications networks and to recognize and promote the people who actually hold a company together.[8]

Culture depends on the attributes of individual human beings and renders a person's slot in the organization chart less important. Stephenson's work offers a different sort of classification that can be integrated with an office plan. One should not, for example, isolate the hubs. Or a manager might decide that a particular job should always be done by someone identified as an effective gatekeeper, and that this person's workplace should be in a boundary area. Thus, it is clear that work like Stephenson's provides an interesting alternative to the traditional hierarchical and work-flow models for designing offices.

Although this work has obvious design implications, it is really a strategy for intervening in the culture through design, among other things. It does not really speak to the ways in which the design itself can help shape the culture. More generally, this work suggests that it might not be necessary for designers to work so hard to embody and symbolize the official corporate structure when the things that really make the company work are structured rather differently.[9]

Office redesigns happen for all sorts of reasons. They are more often driven by the need to accommodate new technologies or by changing business or real-estate market conditions than by a desire to challenge the corporate culture. Nevertheless, nearly all new designs create stress within the culture. Sound studies to help designers and managers understand how design can influence corporate culture in order to benefit the business and the employees are sorely lacking. In fact, although managers often speak as if they had grounds for their decisions, and designers and suppliers offer models, approaches, and slogans, they really have little to go on.

Even when there are solid, research-based findings, managers and designers either remain ignorant of them or speak as if they are. Take, for example, open landscape planning, an approach to office design that is now more than four decades old and still in widespread use. When this approach was developed in Germany four decades ago, its purpose was to facilitate information flow within the office. In the last three decades, the office landscape has become almost universal, for a large number of reasons. Moreover, the adoption of computers, corporate Intranets, the Internet, telecommuting, and a host of other changes have radically transformed the way information is controlled, accessed, and disseminated in the workplace. Yet one can look in recent interior design journals and find designers and executives still speaking about instituting open planning in order to facilitate communication within the office.

There is little research to substantiate this article of faith, and some powerful contrary evidence. As long ago as 1985, Michael Brill and Stephen T. Margulis of BOSTI, a Buffalo-based design research organization, found that ease of communication within an organization depends on having a great deal of privacy, which is still an issue today. Where there is less privacy, they found, there is significantly less communication.[10] When we give this finding a moment's thought, we see that it is not surprising. People are more likely to speak freely if they are convinced that nobody will overhear. Thus, private settings are more likely to produce truthful discussions. Brill and Margulis noted that open office landscapes can be modified with sound-absorbent panels and ambient noise so that the ease of communication approaches that of configurations with private offices. But such measures are ameliorative; they are useful if you prefer open office systems for other reasons.

This study was done before email and internal electronic messaging systems became widespread in offices. Such technology, because it is spontaneous and apparently private, facilitates communication within offices. It does, however, cause

"At the excellent companies the physical configuration of facilities is different. Informality is usually delineated by spartan settings, open doors, fewer walls, and fewer offices. It's hard to imagine a free-flowing exchange of information taking place in the palatial, formal, expensively decorated suites that mark so many corporate or even divisional offices."

Thomas J. Peters and Robert H. Waterman, *In Search of Excellence*, 1982

**New Yorker**, December 6, 1999;
Artist: J. Otto Siebold; Courtesy
J. Otto Siebold and Condé Nast

problems of its own. Because the messages are stored in computers, they create a record that can be subpoenaed and used against the company. As a result, many are trying to tone down the frankness of such messages. Electronic privacy is an illusion.

There are other reasons why companies might wish to install open office systems. They are easier to reconfigure than fixed partitions. They also enable the company to eliminate many of the physical distinctions by which rank has traditionally been expressed, such as office size, carpeting, and finishes. This is a step toward the flattening of management hierarchy that is now considered highly desirable. Because the elements of open systems are, for the most part, considered furniture for tax purposes, they can be depreciated more rapidly than can office walls. Top managers also value the ability to see if workers are busy and whether or not they appear well organized and tidy. Indeed, the fact that open systems discourage frank communication might quiet the sharing of discontent and the hatching of conspiracies, thus giving managers a greater illusion of control. For these reasons, open offices are here to stay. But managers and designers who simply assume that open offices inevitably improve communication are depending on a flimsy, forty-year-old dream.

Though little is known about how physical surroundings influence corporate culture, design is still one of the chief ways in which managers seek to make a difference in the way their companies function. Anyone who has experienced an office redesign knows that this process is one of the most serious crises a corporate culture can face.

In a sense, design is the enemy of culture. Culture evolves; design is imposed. Culture is tacit; design is explicit. Culture values stability; design is radical. Culture is a complex transaction among large numbers of people; designers may consult with workers but, in the end, design is dictatorial. Culture generates deep and arcane knowledge; design wipes out wisdom and forces everyone to start over.

Thus, even people who complain every day about their working conditions feel threatened by the prospect of change. Those who have, over the years, managed to subtly obtain conditions they deem desirable will protest when the almost invisible advantages they so painstakingly won are about to be erased. Workers gather in twos and threes, bemoaning the impact of the changes, forming alliances, developing a strategy of opposition or negotiation. The culture rises to defend itself. Often, this response can have an effect by modifying the redesign or even stopping it. The one thing that all parties in this struggle know is that when managers speak of enhancing the corporate culture, they are actually trying to change it.

It is difficult and painful to change the culture because this means changing the rules and assumptions around which many have based their careers. Office design has long been used to communicate rank and power within an organization. In New York's first Equitable Building, erected in 1870 and generally said to be the first purpose-built corporate headquarters, there were four hundred employees, forty of whom had private offices, many of which contained their own toilets. The rest had to use shared facilities in the basement.[11] Though the Equitable is also said to be the building that first realized the potential of the elevator, the caste distinction between those who had facilities at hand and those who had to go down four flights was quite apparent.

Over the years, such gross differences evolved, at most companies, to an elaborate system of small differences. The size of one's office and its location, window access, number, size, and quality of furnishings, plumbing, and carpet thickness allowed those working in the organization to distinguish between an assistant vice president and a deputy vice president, or between a senior vice president and an executive vice president. Probably more important, it enabled employees to measure their own status and have a sense of their own progress through the hierarchy. During the 1950s and 1960s, suppliers such as carpet manufacturer Bigelow ran an advertising campaign—"A title on the door rates a Bigelow on the floor"—that played to these distinctions. Just as a successful man once hoped to move up from a Pontiac to a Buick and maybe even to a Cadillac, so did the rising executive hope his work surroundings would tell a similar story of progress.

We tend to associate such distinctions with the sack-suit-and-martini era of the postwar decades, but the desire for visible prestige in the workplace has never entirely faded. In the mid-1980s, Brill and Margulis found that 80 percent of the organizations they studied used environmental status markers; they also found that 75 percent of the workers perceived those markers as accurate. Nearly all members of management—those most caught up in the system of status markers—believed them accurate, while the percentage of clerical workers who believed in them was noticeably lower.[12] Whether this was because the clerical workers had a perspective their bosses lacked or whether only the bosses really knew what was going on at the highest echelons isn't clear.

By far, the most desirable status marker identified in the study was gross square footage, though companies themselves were increasingly trying to cut back on that perk and substitute other status symbols. It's not difficult to see why. The point of all these environmental markers is to attest to progress, and those most committed to the system hope that they will progress rapidly. But this is exceedingly expensive. According to the BOSTI data

from the mid-1980s, fully 37 percent of the employees of the companies they studied moved their work location at least once during a given year.[13] (Today, it's an overwhelming 90 percent). If a significant number of these moves were made for reasons of status rather than operational necessity, the costs of communicating the cultural pecking order were high indeed.

Perhaps the most obsessive effort undertaken to deal with the costs of status was the Kevin Roche and John Dinkeloo design for the Union Carbide headquarters in Danbury, Connecticut, which opened in 1983. Unlike most buildings of that period, which consisted primarily of open office landscape systems, this one was based on private offices—the key was that every office had exactly the same dimensions. This office module allowed the architects to create a complex geometry that yielded a large number of pleasant, daylighted offices in a natural-appearing wooded setting.[14] The result was surely one of the most architecturally interesting—albeit unphotogenic—office buildings of the 1980s.

Yet there was something extreme about Union Carbide's reaction to its cultural problem. This seems to have been a corporation fixated on status in the office. The New York headquarters from which it moved had two dozen standard office configurations corresponding to various levels of organizational status. Collapsing such an elaborate system of distinctions into a single office size was tantamount to a cultural revolution, and reveals an obsession with this issue. This was a company whose elaborate internal culture may have prevented it from responding to the culture at large.

The opening of the Danbury building was followed in 1984 by the worst industrial accident in history—at the company's Bhopal, India, insecticide plant—in which more than two thousand people were killed instantly and hundreds of thousands

*A title on the door . . . rates a Bigelow on the floor*

P.S. Is the crowd gathering in your office more and more lately? You'll pack more authority in what you say when you say it on a Bigelow. And that's no fish story, as many a titled executive can tell you. Bigelows are available in special designs, colors and textures. Write for our colorful free brochure on commercial carpets to Bigelow-Sanford, Inc. Dept. A, 140 Madison Avenue, New York 16, N.Y. *People who know . . . buy* BIGELOW.

**Advertisement, Bigelow-Sanford, Inc.;**
c. 1960; Illustrator: Robert Weber;
Courtesy Mohawk International

**Union Carbide headquarters,**
1983; Danbury, Connecticut;
Architect: Kevin Roche John
Dinkeloo and Associates;
Courtesy of the architect

more were injured. An insular corporate culture was one of the reasons critics cited for Union Carbide's poor response to this disaster. In 1999, the company agreed to be acquired by Dow Chemical, making it another of those companies on Whyte's list of firms that moved to a palace in the suburbs to die.

The administration building designed by Frank Lloyd Wright for the Larkin Company in Buffalo can be seen both as an attempt to enshrine a corporate culture and an embodiment of a struggle over its nature. The Larkin Company had been founded as a manufacturer of soap and its earlier offices were, like most offices of manufacturing companies, housed in a wing of the factories. The building Wright designed was necessitated, in large part, by a change in the nature of the company from one that specialized in making things to one that specialized in marketing. The company had evolved from one that sold soap to wholesalers to one that sold gift-boxed soap and related products directly to consumers by mail. Next, the company would use its mailing lists—and its knowledge of customers' buying habits—to sell lamps, desks, oil stoves, and many other high-quality, well-designed products.[15] The prominence of the new office building, in contrast to its predecessor, embodied the emergence of what we would now term an information-driven business.

Wright's six-story structure was organized around an atrium, with offices on balconies whose walls were lined with built-in files that held the cards on which each customer's buying records were kept. The entire building was, in effect, a database, one that could probably now be housed in a single midsized computer. The largely female workforce constantly kept track of this database, processed orders, and wrote correspondence. When Wright wrote and spoke about the building's grimy, factory-district location, he tended to concentrate on the necessity of sending out clean-looking letters from a dirty place, but creating a clean and respectable environment for the female workers was also extremely important. The result was a building with few windows on the outside, illuminated largely by daylight from the atrium. It was an early attempt to create an office building that seemed to be a world of its own, safe from what was outside.

Built at a time when people were less reticent about attempting a concrete expression of values, and given that several of the company's leaders were devotees of the Arts and Crafts movement, it isn't surprising that the exterior of the building contained a number of allegorical sculptures, reliefs, and inspirational sayings. On the interior, though, the expression of values was not insistent. The words written on the sides of the balconies were not mottoes or quotations but rather the raw materials from which the workers in the building could construct their own inspirational maxims. The words were written in groups of three: "Intelligence Enthusiasm Control," "Cooperation Energy Industry," "Thought Feeling Air." One executive said the words were intended "to encourage independence of thought."[16]

Wright's chief client, Darwin Martin, the manager largely responsible for the company's expansion into mail-order sales, was not a member of the Larkin family. Still owning the company, the family identified most strongly with the manufacturing rather than the marketing end of the operation. The Larkins had their offices in the entrance annex of Wright's building, the same location where one would expect to find a front office in any manufacturing facility.[17] Martin's office was open, and in the very center of the atrium, with the activity and information all around him. It is tempting to see the design of the building, in which these two power centers each get their own sculptural form, as an embodiment of a struggle over the nature of the company. It is also tempting to see this as a struggle in which the future of the office building—managerial, information based, marketing oriented, and geared toward the recruitment and retention of a high-quality workforce—faced off against the old enclosed, controlling, manufacturing-oriented proprietary model. In this case, the future did not triumph over the past. Martin was eventually forced out of the company, and its information-intensive marketing model was probably ahead of its time.

Wright's design seems to have been quite popular with the workers. They had complaints on some of the chairs he designed, but the consensus seems to have been that it was an excellent place in which to work.

The Larkin Building was, like the Union Carbide headquarters, an exceptional office building. This is not simply because it was aesthetically distinguished but because both its exterior and interiors were shaped by a specific way of doing business. When the Larkin Building was erected, the pattern of office buildings as ornamented containers for neutral space was already established. Even buildings erected by large companies primarily for their own use contained floors—often the most desirable ones—intended to be rented out to tenants. This means most offices occupy space that is more or less generic and, unlike the Larkin Building, there is little relationship between the exterior and what happens inside.

Ever since the first Equitable Building, where law firms were willing to pay top dollar for the most desirable space, urban headquarters buildings have been designed with tenants in mind. Even Philadelphia's famous PSFS Building (1932)—whose modernist exterior was elaborated even more brilliantly in the interior banking floors, safe deposit rooms, doorknobs, and office wastebaskets—was nevertheless designed to accommodate tenants. One of its most innovative features, a movable partition system that allowed offices reconfigured for new tenants virtually overnight, was a direct ancestor of today's office system.[18]

An expressive building like Wright's might be aesthetically pleasing, but if its design is too closely tied to a particular way of doing things, the building is irresponsible. That's because technologies and modes of organization—not to mention corporate ownership—change rapidly. One can expect a building to contain many ways of doing things, and many cultures, during its economic life.

The strongest example of this change I have ever encountered is in a building in Radnor, Pennsylvania, on the Main Line outside Philadelphia. My first visit was in 1979, when it had just opened as the headquarters for the Sun Companies. This five-story building, set amid rolling hills, seemed more to have been built for a modern-day Sun King. A sense of the culture that was being encouraged was apparent as one walked through the door, encountered the gilded security desk, and looked into the five-story atrium: Courtiers only.

Lush carpeting, fine paneling, and stone accents were used throughout the building. The most expensive element of an office building, however, is not materials but space itself, and this was expended lavishly. As one ascended in the building, the secretaries' desks moved farther apart and the offices became ever larger, until one reached the top level and the exalted presence of the CEO.

Even at the time, it was evident that the authoritarian culture that the design seemed to reflect was an anachronism. This was not, however, a culture left over from an earlier time. Rather, it was something new. Sun had, for most of its history, been a closely held second-tier oil company, with a penurious reputation quite at odds with the corporate profligacy then on display. But during the 1970s, petroleum ruled, and Sun redefined itself as a family of companies involved in refining, marketing, real estate, shipping, and other assorted ventures far removed from the gas station. It was, suddenly, an empire, and an imperial command center seemed to be required.

Was it the culture that failed? I don't know. But a culture cannot survive if it is at odds with the realities of the outside world and, during the 1980s, it became apparent that the oil age was over. Sun gradually shrank back to what it had been. Imperial days were but a memory; eventually, the company moved to much smaller space in downtown Philadelphia.

When I returned to the building in 1994, I did not, at first, remember that I had been there before—everything was so very different. Much of the ground floor had been rented to the KMPG–Peat Marwick consulting firm, and it was one of the first full-scale examples of hoteling. Because employees often work for weeks at a time at their clients' sites, they have no need for a permanent home office. When they need an office, they call to make a reservation, and the files they need, along with family pictures and other personalizing elements, are brought to an available cubicle. This intense use of space could not have been more different from the luxurious spaciousness found in the building when it was the Sun headquarters.

The most shocking scene of all was in the atrium, which was once so powerfully empty. It was now filled with tables shaded by large canvas umbrellas. But this was not a café; the tables were occupied by people laboring away at laptops. These people were, I was told, "moteling." They hadn't called for a reservation, had called too late, or required only a short time in the office. The umbrellas weren't there to lend a festive air; they had been installed to reduce the glare of the skylights on the screens of the laptops. One can scarcely imagine what sort of a culture could develop here. Nobody is around long enough to know anyone else. This

marks the end of the course of corporate empires—postcultural.

The BOSTI team found that office workers actually prefer their workplaces to be devoid of strong color.[19] They like neutrality, perhaps because they recognize that if a strong taste is expressed in the space, it won't be theirs. More likely, it will be that of a top executive who confuses his own quirks with the personality of the entire company.

Because those deciding which office designs are published have a natural bias against visual neutrality, the designs remembered are likely to be those in which a strong executive is actively trying to use design to shape culture. Though the aims are often clearly legible in the space, this visual clarity does not necessarily mean that the design succeeded in its intention.

On this basis, there was probably no more celebrated group of offices in recent years than those designed for the Chiat/Day advertising agency in both Los Angeles and New York between 1986 and 1994. The imagery of an office in which nothing is fixed and everything is temporary and open represented an extreme case of a growing trend. The thought of having to duck into an old Tilt-a-Whirl car to have a private telephone call, as was the case at the second Los Angeles office, became an emblem of the terrifying contingency of modern work life.

These offices reflected the thinking of Jay Chiat, former owner of the agency, who decided, he said, "that if we made the office a place, rather than just a place to store stuff, it would be more valuable."[20] This is a goal similar to that which underlies hoteling, as at the KMPG–Peat Marwick office.

Chiat, however, was less interested in reducing his fixed real-estate costs than he was in changing his workforce. "I was really tired of working with all these business people that I kept having to tell what to do," he said. "I thought it would be great to work with intelligent people that you could give an assign-

**Chiat/Day offices,** 1994;
New York, New York;
Architect: Gaetano Pesce;
Photographer: Francesco Radino;
Courtesy ECIFFO

Chiat/Day office, 1986;
Venice, California;
Architect: Frank Gehry and Associates;
Photographer: Francesco Radino;
Courtesy ECIFFO

# alternative officing

| | | |
|---|---|---|
| **high technology** | | 50% TELECOMMUTING<br>37% VIRTUAL OFFICING<br>15% HOTELING |
| **insurance companies** | | 43% TELECOMMUTING<br>25% VIRTUAL OFFICING<br>8% HOTELING |
| **consulting firms** | *high* | 33% TELECOMMUTING<br>31% VIRTUAL OFFICING<br>11% HOTELING |
| **non-profit organizations** | *moderate* | 23% TELECOMMUTING<br>10% VIRTUAL OFFICING<br>1% HOTELING |
| **legal services** | *low* | 16% TELECOMMUTING<br>12% VIRTUAL OFFICING<br>3% HOTELING |
| **real-estate firms** | | 17% TELECOMMUTING<br>11% VIRTUAL OFFICING<br>2% HOTELING |

Different types of businesses have adopted "alternative officing" in varying degrees. Source: "What Office Tenants Want" (1999), Building Owners and Managers Association and Urban Land Institute

ment, give them parameters, then they'd go off, do the research and come back with the completed assignment." His model was a university, which provides libraries and other resources for the students but does not monitor where or when students do their work.

"The new concept of the office changed the way we looked at people," Chiat said, "and in the end, the result was a group of people who were now able to operate independently and people who were more capable of taking control over their personal freedom that I don't think you can get from working in a traditional hierarchical environment." It's important to note that, in many cases, employees who were uncomfortable not knowing where to go when they came to work in the morning either quit or found other jobs. Those who liked working in this way were drawn to the agency. Advertising has traditionally been an unstable business, with people arriving and leaving all the time, so this approach may not have been as threatening there as it would in more traditional businesses such as insurance, banking, and law.

Chiat has since sold the agency, and the offices have moved into more conventional places. Chiat's premise—that design can shape a creative culture—has, nevertheless, been influential, especially among dot-com startups in New York's downtown Silicon Alley.

The businesses that create such spaces are not involved in processing information according to an industrial model, as one finds in the insurance or banking industries. Rather, their offices are about bringing people together so that they can generate and refine ideas for an ever-accelerating entertainment and consumer culture. For a start-up, creating

an atmosphere that reflects the kind of thinking you want to encourage makes sense. If the design reflects the values and feelings of the business, it also helps to draw the sort of staff who will be comfortable working there.

There are also pragmatic reasons for concentrating on collective work areas rather than individual workstations. Many new companies in entertainment and electronic commerce don't know how many people they will be hiring or what those people's jobs will be. To concentrate on places where people gather and generate ideas together is actually a prudent course for a business that has little capital and not much more than potential.

Thus, many of the offices published today depart from the quasi-military organization characteristic of the post-World War II era and have taken on the aura of a progressive kindergarten. How many of these lively designs actually spawn cultures that generate good ideas and have the ability to follow through on them is impossible to know. But they do, perhaps, breed a kind of worker who is more comfortable with instability than was the fellow with the walnut paneling and the Bigelow carpet. Such places reflect the fact that offices no longer have a monopoly on information or communication. The office may someday be just a place to meet, or a place to go when you need to get out of the house.

It is easy to laugh at the mid-twentieth-century office, with its complex codes of status, but it was a place that encouraged workers to believe they were making a career. These new offices, filled with young people whose payment consists largely of stock options, are for workers savvy enough to know that they are merely making a bet.

**Chill-Out Room at 11600 Sunrise Valley Drive,** 2000; Reston, Virginia; Architect: Stanmyre Noel Architects; Photographer: Steven Brooke

The chill-out room is one of many amenities offered by this building's developer, the Morino Group. Others include an indoor basketball court, café, fitness center, outdoor volleyball court, jogging trail, and party pavilion. While such benefits are common at large companies or owner-occupied buildings, they are unusual in speculative projects such as this one, which houses emerging Internet businesses and private equity firms.

1. In 1994 and 1995, working as a consultant to Time Warner Electronic Publications as multimedia editor of *Bartlett's Familiar Quotations*, I several times found myself in the crossfire between the Time and Warner cultures that were still evident years after that earlier megamerger.

2. Joseph Heller, *Something Happened* (New York: Alfred A. Knopf, 1974), 13.

3. Edgar H. Schein, *The Corporate Culture Survival Guide* (San Francisco: Jossey-Bass, 1999), 21.

4. See *Interior Design* 70, no. 6 (May 1999): 256.

5. The observations in this paragraph and the preceding one are based largely on an interview with Patricia Conway, a longtime designer of corporate interiors who is working on a book about office design.

6. William H. Whyte, *City: Rediscovering the Center* (New York: Doubleday, 1988), 294–95.

7. Pasquale Gagliardi, *Symbols and Artifacts: Views of the Corporate Landscape* (Berlin: Walter de Gruyter, 1990), 6.

8. See for example, Eleena De Lisser, "The Corporate Jungle," in *Wall Street Journal* (September 28, 1998): 1-B.

9. Schein and others have criticized work like Stephenson's as mechanistic and reductive, because it attempts to analyze diverse cultures using a single, simple model that can be incorporated into a software program. One reason for the attractiveness of Stephenson's approach to some managers is that it offers some operational guidance for design and other matters that others in the field ignore.

10. Michael Brill, with Stephen T. Margulis and BOSTI, *Using Office Design to Increase Productivity,* vol. 2 (Buffalo, N.Y.: Workplace Design & Productivity, Inc., 1985), 54.

11. Patricia Conway, "The Equitable Chronicles," in *Wharton Real Estate Journal* 1, no. 1 (Spring 1997): 37.

12. Brill, *Using Office Design*, 60.

13. Ibid., 67.

14. Andrea O. Dean, "Corporate Contrast in the Suburbs" in *Architecture* 74 no. 2 (1985): 62–69.

15. Jack Quinan, *Frank Lloyd Wright's Larkin Building: Myth and Fact* (New York: Architectural History Foundation, 1987), 9–14.

16. Ibid., 93.

17. Ibid., 38.

18. A paradox of the PSFS Building was that it was a revolutionary edifice for a conservative institution whose success rested on small savers who never moved their money. Viewed closely, the building communicated substance as clearly as any of the templelike strongboxes of previous generations, and the corporate culture prized continuity. There was even an architect on staff whose full-time job was to ensure that the integrity of the building would be respected. The institution failed when it abandoned its conservative roots and engaged in more speculative endeavors.

    The building was recently converted to a hotel, after it was determined that its small floor plates were not suitable for contemporary office tenants who like large horizontal expanses. In Europe, where access to windows is expected and even required by law in some areas, the PSFS would be a viable shape. This is another manifestation of cultural difference in office building design.

19. Brill, *Using Office Design*, 62.

20. All Chiat quotations are taken from Marilyn Zelinsky, *New Workplaces for New Workstyles* (New York: McGraw-Hill, 1997), 72–73.

# epilogue

## new american boomtown

Steven Brooke's essay on the Dulles High-Tech Corridor, outside Washington, D.C., in northern Virginia, was specially commissioned for *On the Job* and photographed in the spring of 2000. It offers a unique perspective on one of the newest and fastest-growing office landscapes in America. Office buildings, residences, hotels, and shopping malls whiz by motorists as they travel along the corridor's main artery, Route 267, as it connects Tysons Corner, Virginia, and Dulles International Airport. (This local architectural icon, pictured left, was designed by the office of Eero Saarinen and completed in 1962.) A beneficiary of Cold War technology transfers and the state's pro-business attitude, the area houses such "digital economy" companies as America Online, Teligent, and MicroStrategy, as well as financial giants like Freddie Mac. Between 1992 and 1999, office space in this part of northern Virginia sprawled from 20 million square feet to 100 million. Even more staggering is the employment figure for high-tech workers in the Washington area, which now surpasses federal employment. The landscape of the corridor fuses the dense urbanism and pastoral suburbanism presented in the photo essay "High-Modern Moment" that opens this book. Unlike that essay's celebration of corporate palazzos, Brooke's essay documents the rush and transience of a new boomtown of mainly speculative office buildings, where, according to one keen observer who works in the area, "it's what's on the screen that counts." In the corridor, as in the "new economy," companies come and go with the speed of a computer's delete button.

—D.A., C.B.B.

# business terminology index

In 1965, Frank M. Knox included this index of business terminology in *The Knox Standard Guide to Design and Control of Business Forms* (McGraw-Hill). The scope of the index underscores the complexity of the business world and office culture as well as the American obsession with specialized terminology. Knox also authored *The How and Why of Pay Roll Records* (1946) and *Managing Paperwork: A Key to Productivity* (1980).
—D.A., C.B.B.

To try to establish a Functional Index of forms based on subjects, operations or conditions, and functions requires, first, that those terms be defined in themselves. The following definitions have been taken from the author's *Dictionary of Standard Forms Terminology.*

### SUBJECT
That concerning which anything is said or done; thing or person treated of; matter; theme; topic. In forms control, the subject becomes the matter or thing in relation to which an action takes place or to which a condition refers.

### OPERATION
In general, act, process, or effect of operating. A doing of performing action; work. In forms control, the operation represents the action which takes place in relation to the subject.

### CONDITION
A mode or state of being. In forms control, the condition refers to the state in which the subject may be at any time.

### FUNCTION
The natural or characteristic purpose of a thing: that purpose which the thing or person is supposed to accomplish or fulfill. Some dictionaries define "function" in terms of an "action," whereas others use the term "purpose," which fits better into this classification and is, therefore, used.

In each case the subject is expressed by a noun; operation and condition are noun phrases referring to either a verb or an adjective, and the function is expressed by an infinitive. Unless the classification of any given form can be so expressed, it should be questioned since the entire purpose of the classification of forms into the Index is to simplify and make clear a confusing situation. A definitive list of subjects, operations and conditions, and functions as developed by the writer over many years is as follows:

## SUBJECTS

Accident (see also "injury-illness" and "damages")

Account:

Accounts receivable

Accounts payable

Account general

Action (for general use only, be specific when possible)

Address

Analysis (make careful distinction between "analysis" as a subject and "analysis" as an operation)

Applicant

Appointment (distinguish between "appointment" as a subject and "appointment" as an operation)

Appropriation

Assets

Assured (use "insured")

Audit (can also be used as an operation)

Award

Bad debt

Bank account

Bank check

Beneficiary

Benefit plan

Benefits (careful distinction between the plan and the benefits must be made)

Bid

Blueprint (use "prints" instead)

Book

Budget

Building (can use combined term "land and buildings")

Burden (see also "overhead")

Call, sales

Candidate

Cargo

Carrier (applies in "insurance" rather than in "transportation")

Cash (see also "earnings")

Certificate

Charges (do not confuse with "costs")

Check (see also "bank check")

Claim (do not confuse with "loss" in insurance)

Classification

Commission (easily confused with "earnings" and "cash")

Committee

Communication

Complaints trouble

Container

Contribution

Correspondence (do not confuse with "communication")

Costs

Credit (can also be used as an operation)

Curriculum

Customer

Customer service

Damages (can also be used as a condition)

Demurrage

Department

Deposit (can also be used as an operation)

Depreciation

Dictation

Die

Distributor

Dividend

Documents (easily confused with "correspondence," "records," etc.)

Drawing

Drilling

Dues

Duty

Earnings (must be carefully distinguished from "cash")

Education

Electrotype

Employee (must be carefully distinguished from "employment")

Employment

Endorsement

Entertainment

Estimate

Event

Experience

Facility

File

Fingerprint

Food

Forecast

Forms (must be carefully distinguished from "records," "documents," etc.)

Formula

Freight

Funds (see also "cash")

Garnishment

Gauge

Grievance

Hazard

Hearing

Housing

Income

Indemnity

Injury-illness

Inquiry

Instructor

Insurance (be very careful not to make a catch-all)

Insured

Interest

Invention

Inventory

Investment

Job

Key

Labor (must be carefully distinguished from "work")

Land and buildings

Law

Lawsuit

Lease

Ledger

License

Lien

List

Loan

Loss (must be carefully distinguished from "claim")

Machinery and equipment

Mail

Mailing list

Market

Materials and supplies (either one alone is too difficult to identify)

Meal

Medical examination

Medicine

Meeting

Member

Membership

Merchandise

Messenger service

Model

Mold

Money (must be carefully distinguished from "cash")

Name

Nows

Notice

Office supplies

Order

Organization (can also be used as an operation)

Overhead

Overtime

Package

Part

Passport

Patent

Patient

Pattern

Payroll

Pension

Person

Personal property

Plant

Policy

Postage

Premises

Premium

Price

Prints

Problem

Procedure

Product

Production (do not confuse with "job," "work," "work-in-process," etc.)

Profit and loss

Program

Project

Property

Prospects

Publication

Purchase (can also be used as an operation)

Quotation

Railroad car

Rate

Real estate

Recipe

Records (do not confuse with "forms," "documents," etc.)

Recreation

Regulation

Rent

Report (must be carefully distinguished from "records")

Reservation

Reserve

Resolution

Returnable container

Revenue (must be carefully distinguished from "cash," "earnings," etc.)

Rights

Room

Royalties

Rubbish

Rules and regulations

Selective service

Semifinished parts (do not confuse with "work-in-progress")

Service

Shipment

Signature

Social security

Specifications (can also be used as a condition)

Specimen

Standard

Standard practice

Stock (do not confuse with "securities")

Student

Suggestion

Supplier

Tariff

Tax

Telegram

Telephone message

Teletype (should use "communication")

Ticket

Time

Title

Tool (distinguish between "tool" and "equipment-machinery")

Trademark

Training

Transportation (can also be used as an operation)

Travel

Trouble

Tuition

Utilities

Vacation

Vehicle

Vendor

Visa

Visitor

Wages (distinguish between "wages" and "income")

Waiter's check

Weather

Work (do not confuse with "production" and "work-in-process")

Work-in-process

## OPERATIONS AND CONDITIONS

Absence of

Acceptance-rejection of

Addition to

Adherence to

Adjustment-correction of

Admission of

Aging of

Allocation of

Analysis of (must be carefully distinguished from "inspection of" and "examination of")

Application for

Appointment of

Appraisal of

Appropriation of

Attendance of

Audit of

Availability of


Back-order of

Birth of

Budget of


Calibration of

Cancellation of

Certification of (can also be a function)

Change of

Charge-off of

Citizenship of

Classification of

Clearance of

Collection of

Completion of

Computation of (can also be a function)

Condition of (do not confuse with "status of")

Correction of

Correctness of

Cost of

Coverage of

Credit of (or "credit to")


Damage to

Death of

Debit-credit to

Deduction of

Deferment of

Delay of

Delinquency of

Delivery of (do not confuse with "transportation of" and "shipping of")

Demonstration of

Departure of

Deposit of

Depreciation of

Design of

Destination of

Destruction of

Development of

Disbursement of (usually included in "payment of")

Discount of

Disposition of

Distribution of


Efficiency of

Employment of

Examination of (must be carefully distinguished from "analysis of" and "inspection of")

Exemption of

Expiration of

Exportation of

Extension of


Filling of


Garnishment of (can also be used as a subject)


Handling of

Housing of


Identification of

Incorrectness of

Indoctrination of

Information about (use as sparingly as possible)

Inspection of

Installation of

Instruction of

Insurance of (must be carefully distinguished from subject "insurance")

Interview of

Investigation of (must be carefully distinguished from "examination of," etc.)

Issuance of

Lease of

Limitation of

Listing of

Loading of (check against "shipping of")

Loan of

Location of

Loss of

Lost and found (can also be used as a subject)


Manufacture of

Marriage of

Minutes of

Movement of


Obsolescence of

Opening of

Operation of

Organization of

Orientation of

Overage of

Overage shortage of

Ownership of


Packaging of (must be carefully distinguished from "shipping of")

Passage of

Payment of

Placement of

Prevention of

Price of

Procurement of (check against the general subject "purchase")

Properties of

Protection from


Qualification of


Rate of (can also appear as a subject)

Rating of

Recall of

Receipt of

Reconciliation of

Recovery of

Refund of

Reinstatement of

Rejection of

Release of

Rental of (must be carefully distinguished from "rent" as a subject)

Repair maintenance of

Replenishment of

Reprimand of

Requirements of

Reservation of

Retention of

Return of

Rework of (must be carefully distinguished from "work-in-process")

Rooming of

Routing of


Seniority of

Settlement of

Setup of

Shipping of (must be carefully distinguished from "transportation of")

Shortage of

Shrinkage of

Shutdown of

Specifications of

Status of

Stocking of

Storage of

Substitution of

Switching of


Termination of

Testing of

Training of

Transfer of

Transmittal of

Transportation of

Treatment of


Use of


Vacancy of

Value of

Variance of

Verification of

Violation of


Weight of

Withdrawal of

Withholding of

## FUNCTIONS

In endeavoring to identify and define the functions of paperwork for the practical classification of forms in a Functional Index, two problems arise: first, the definition of the word "function" itself and, second, the treatment of words that are, to some degree or other, synonymous with each other. The following treatment has been found to be workable beyond any other in the practical working out of the problem.

### The Eighteen Essential Functions

**To acknowledge**
**To agree**
**To apply**
**To authorize**
**To cancel**
**To certify**
**To claim**
**To estimate**
**To follow up**
**To identify**
**To instruct**
**To notify**
**To order**
**To record**
**To report**
**To request**
**To route**
**To schedule**

## SYNONYMS TO BE AVOIDED AND ALTERNATIVES TO BE USED IN THEIR PLACES

| | |
|---|---|
| **Abolish** | To cancel |
| **Accept** | To acknowledge |
| **Account** | To report |
| **Agree** | To certify |
| **Allow** | To authorize |
| **Annul** | To cancel |
| **Apply** | To request |
| **Appraise** | To estimate |
| **Ask** | To request |
| **Attest** | To certify |
| **Calculate** | To estimate |
| **Commission** | To authorize |
| **Compute** | To estimate |
| **Confirm** | To certify |
| **Consent** | To agree |
| **Contract** | To agree |
| **Demand** | To claim |
| **Endorse** | To certify |
| **Establish** | To identify |
| **Grant** | To acknowledge |
| **Guarantee** | To certify |
| **Inform** | To notify |
| **Inquire** | To request |
| **Instruct** | To order |
| **Inventory** | To report |
| **Invoice** | To notify |
| **Permit** | To authorize |
| **Promise** | To agree |
| **Question** | To request |
| **Recall** | To cancel |
| **Receipt** | To acknowledge |
| **Regulate** | To order |
| **Repeal** | To cancel |
| **Report** | To notify |
| **Requisition** | To request |
| **Rule** | To order |
| **Tell** | To report |
| **Testify** | To certify |
| **Transmit** | To route |
| **Validate** | To acknowledge |
| **Verify** | To certify |
| **Warn** | To notify |

# selected bibliography

Abercrombie, Stanley. *George Nelson*. Cambridge: MIT Press, 1995.

Abercrombie, Stanley. *A Philosophy of Interior Design*. New York: Harper & Row, 1990.

Abercrombie, Stanley. Introduction to *Work, Life, Tools*. New York: Monacelli Press and Steelcase Design Partnership, 1997.

Adams, Scott. *Journey to Cubeville*. Kansas City, Kan.: Andrews McMeel, 1998.

Alvesson, Mats. *Corporate Culture and Organizational Symbolism*: *An Overview*. Berlin and New York: Walter de Gruyter, 1992.

*Architectural Record:* Prominent recent coverage of innovative workplace designs includes June 1989, June 1992, June 1994, October 1995, December 1996, June 1997, January 1998, and *Business Week/Architectural Record* Good Design Is Good Business awards in October 1997, 1998, 1999, 2000.

*Architecture 3s: Pioneering British High Tech*. London: Phaidon, 1999.

Aron, Cindy Sondik. *Ladies and Gentleman of the Civil Service: Middle-class Workers in Victorian America*. New York: Oxford University Press, 1987.

Austrian, Geoffrey D. *Herman Hollerith: Forgotten Giant of Information Processing*. New York: Columbia University Press, 1982.

Banham, Reyner. *The Architecture of the Well-Tempered Environment*. 2nd ed. Chicago: University of Chicago Press, 1969.

Becker, Franklin. *The Total Workplace*. New York: Van Nostrand Reinhold, 1990.

Becker, Franklin, and Fritz Steele. *Workplace by Design: Mapping the High-Performance Workscape*. San Francisco: Jossey-Bass, 1995.

Bedini, Silvio A. *Thomas Jefferson and His Copying Machines*. Charlottesville: University of Virginia Press, 1984.

Bluestone, Daniel. *Constructing Chicago*. New Haven, Conn.: Yale University Press, 1991.

Brand, Stewart. *How Buildings Learn*. New York: Viking, 1994.

Brandt, Peter B. *Office Design*. New York: Whitney Library of Design, 1992.

Brill, Michael, Stephen T. Margulis, and BOSTI. *Using Office Design to Increase Productivity,* vol. 2. Buffalo, N.Y.: Workplace Design & Productivity, Inc., 1985.

Brooks, John. *Telephone: The First One Hundred Years*. New York: Harper & Row, 1976.

Caplan, Ralph. *The Design of Herman Miller*. New York: Whitney Library of Design, 1976.

Carron, Christian G. *Grand Rapids Furniture: The Story of Amercia's Furniture City*. Grand Rapids, Mich.: The Public Museum of Grand Rapids, 1998.

Chandler, Alfred D. *The Visible Hand: The Managerial Revolution in American Business*. Cambridge, Mass.: Belknap Press, 1977.

Conway, Patricia. "The Equitable Chronicles." *Wharton Real Estate Journal* 1, no. 1. (Spring 1997).

Croly, Herbert. *The Promise of American Life*. New York: MacMillan, 1909.

Diamond, Michael A. *The Unconscious Life of Organizations: Interpreting Organizational Identity*. Westport, Conn.: Quorum Books, 1993.

Duffy, Francis. *The Changing Workplace*. London: Phaidon, 1992.

Duffy, Francis. *The New Office*. London: Conran Octopus, 1997.

*Everybody's Business: A Fund of Retrievable Ideas for Humanizing Life in the Office*. Zeeland, Mich.: Herman Miller Research Corporation, 1985.

Gagliardi, Pasquale, ed. *Symbols and Artifacts: Views of the Corporate Landscape*. Berlin and New York: Walter de Gruyter, 1990.

Galbraith, John Kenneth. *The Affluent Society*. Boston: Houghton Mifflin, 1958.

Galbraith, John Kenneth. *The New Industrial State*. Boston: Houghton Mifflin, 1967.

Godley, Andrew, and Oliver M. Westall. *Business History and Business Culture*. Manchester, UK: Manchester University Press, 1996.

Goldberg, Alfred. *The Pentagon: The First Fifty Years*. Washington, D.C.: Historical Office, Office of the Secretary of Defense, 1992.

Haber, Samuel. *Efficiency and Uplift: Scientific Management in the Progressive Era, 1880-1920*. Chicago: University of Chicago Press, 1964.

Hammer, Michael, and James Champy. *Reengineering the Corporation*. New York: HarperBusiness, 1993.

Hartkopf, Volker, Vivian Loftness, Pleasantine Drake, Fred Dubin, Peter A.D. Mill, and George R. Ziga. *Designing the Office of the Future: The Japanese Approach to Tomorrow's Workplace*. New York: John Wiley & Sons, 1993.

Heller, Joseph. *Something Happened*. New York: Alfred A. Knopf, 1974.

Hohl, Reinhold. *Office Buildings: An International Survey*. New York: Praeger, 1968.

Howard, Robert. *Brave New Workplace*. New York: Penguin, 1985.

Hughes, Thomas P. *Rescuing Prometheus*. New York: Pantheon, 1998.

Iannacci, Anthony, ed. *Developing the Architecture of the Workplace: Gensler 1967-1997*. New York: Edizioni Press, 1998.

The Impact of Office Environment on Productivity and Quality of Working Life. Buffalo, N.Y.: BOSTI, 1981.

Jackson, Vincent E. Modern Office Appliances. 3rd ed. London: Macdonald and Evans, 1936.

Johnston, Edna. "Rendering a Permanent Service": Organized Labor and Federal Workers, 1900–1932. Dissertation presented to the faculty of the University of Virginia, forthcoming.

Jordan, Ann T., ed. Practicing Anthropology in Corporate America. Arlington, Va.: National Association for the Practice of Anthropology, 1994.

Kakar, Sudhir. Frederick Taylor: A Study in Personality and Innovation. Cambridge, Mass.: MIT Press, 1970.

Kessler-Harris, Alice. Out of Work: A History of Wage-Earning Women in the United States. New York: Oxford University Press, 1982.

Knobel, Lance. Office Furniture: Twentieth-Century Design. New York: E.P. Dutton, 1987.

Kotter, J.P., and J.F. Heskett. Corporate Culture and Performance. New York: Free Press, 1992.

Kouwenhoven, John A. Made in America: The Arts in Modern Civilization. 1948. Reprint, Garden City, N.Y.: Doubleday, 1962.

Kron, Joan, and Suzanne Slesin. High Tech: The Industrial Style and Sourcebook for the Home. New York: Clarkson Potter, 1978.

Levy, Steven. Hackers: Heroes of the Computer Revolution. Garden City, N.Y.: Anchor Press/Doubleday, 1984.

Lewis, Arthur O., Jr., ed. Of Men and Machines. New York: E.P. Dutton, 1963.

"The Liberated, Exploited, Pampered, Frazzled, Uneasy New American Worker." New York Times Magazine (March 5, 2000).

Guiheux, Alain. Lieux? De Travail. Exhibition catalogue, Paris: Centre Georges Pompidou, 1986.

Lipman, Jonathan. Frank Lloyd Wright and the Johnson Wax Buildings, New York: Rizzoli, 1986.

Loftness, Vivian, and Volker Hartkopf, Susan Nurge, and Derek Rubinoff. "Beyond the Open Plan: Space Planning Concepts to Sort Organizational, Technical, and Environmnetal Change." Center for Building Performance and Diagnostics, Carnegie Mellon University (Spring 1994).

Marberry, Sara O. Color in the Office: Design Trends from 1950-1990 and Beyond. New York: Van Nostrand Reinhold, 1994.

Marchand, Roland. Advertising the American Dream: Making Way for Modernity, 1920-1940. Berkeley: University of California Press, 1985.

Martin, Reinhold. Architecture and Organization: USA, c. 1956. Dissertation presented to the faculty of Princeton University, 1999.

McLuhan, Marshall. Understanding Media: The Extensions of Man. New York: McGraw-Hill, 1964.

Mumford, Lewis. Art and Technics. New York: Columbia University Press, 1952.

Mumford, Lewis. Technics and Civilization. New York: Harcourt Brace, 1934.

Myerson, Jeremy, and Philip Ross. The Creative Office. Corte Madera, Calif.: Gingko Press, 1999.

Patton, Phil. "The Virtual Office Becomes Reality." New York Times (October 28, 1993).

Patton, Phil. Made in USA: The Secret Histories of the Things That Made America. New York: Grove-Weidenfeld, 1992.

Pélegrin-Genel, Élisabeth. The Office. Paris: Flammarion, 1996.

Peters, Tom, and Robert H. Waterman. In Search of Excellence: Lessons from America's Best-Run Corporations. New York: Warner, 1982.

Pile, John F. Open Office Planning: A Handbook for Interior Designers and Architects. New York: Whitney Library of Design, 1978.

Propst, Robert. The Office: A Facility Based on Change. Elmhurst, Ill.: Business Press, 1968.

Pulgram, William L., and Richard E. Stonis. Designing the Automated Office. New York: Whitney Library of Design, 1978.

Quinan, Jack. Frank Lloyd Wright's Larkin Building: Myth and Fact. New York and Cambridge: Architectural History Foundation and MIT Press, 1987.

Rheingold, Howard. Tools for Thought. New York: Simon & Schuster, 1985.

Russell, James S. "Emblems of Modernism or Machine-Age Dinosaurs?" Architectural Record 177 (June 1989).

Russell, James S. "A Company Headquarters Planned for Flexibility." New York Times (September 7, 1998).

Sampson, Anthony. Company Man: The Rise and Fall of Corporate Life. New York: Times Business/Random House, 1995.

Saphier, Michael. Office Planning and Design. New York: McGraw-Hill, 1968.

Schein, Edgar H. The Corporate Culture Survival Guide. San Francisco: Jossey-Bass, 1999.

Schein, Edgar H. Organizational Culture and Leadership. 2nd ed. San Francisco: Jossey-Bass, 1992.

Schlereth, Thomas J. Victorian America: Transformations in Everyday Life, 1876-1915. New York: HarperCollins, 1991.

Schulze, J. William. The American Office: Its Organization, Management and Records. 2nd ed. New York: Ronald Press Company, 1914.

Shultz, Earle, and Walter Simmons. Offices in the Sky. Indianapolis: Bobbs-Merrill, 1959.

Standage, Tom. The Victorian Internet: The Remarkable Story of the Telegraph and the Nineteenth Century's On-Line Pioneers. New York: Walker, 1998.

Steelcase: The First 75 Years. Grand Rapids, Mich.: Steelcase, Inc., 1987.

Studios Architecture: The Power of the Pragmatic. Milan: L'Arca Edizioni, 1999.

Sundstrom, Eric. Work Places: The Psychology of the Physical Environment in Offices and Factories. New York: Cambridge University Press, 1986.

Sutherland, Daniel E. The Expansion of Everyday Life, 1860-1876. New York: Harper & Row, 1989.

Taylor, Frederick Winslow. The Principles of Scientific Management. New York: Harper, 1911.

Tetlow, Karin. The New Office: Designs for Corporations, People & Technology. Glen Cove, NY: PBC/Architecture & Interior Design, 1996.

Turner, Barry R., ed. Organizational Symbolism. Berlin: Walter de Gruyter, 1989.

Utt, Florence M. The Receptionist in a Large or Small Organization. Detroit, Mich.: Florence Utt Schools, 1959.

Veldhoen, Erik, and Bart Piepers. The Demise of the Office. Rotterdam: Uitgeverij, 1995.

Wharton, P.G., I.O. Royse, Harold C. Pennicke, Harry A. Snow, Allen Everett, and Norman C. Firth. Office Machines and Methods. New York: American Management Association, 1935.

Whitely, Richard C. The Customer-Driven Company. New York: Addison-Wesley, 1991.

Whyte, William H. City: Rediscovering the Center. New York: Doubleday, 1988.

Whyte, William H. The Organization Man. New York: Simon & Shuster, 1956.

Willis, Carol. Form Follows Finance: Skyscrapers and Skylines in New York and Chicago. New York: Princeton Architectural Press: 1995.

Williams, Cecil, David Armstrong, and Clark Malcolm. The Negotiable Environment: People, White-Collar Work, and the Office. Ann Arbor, Mich.: Facility Management Institute, 1985.

Wineman, Jean D. Behavioral Issues in Office Design. New York: Van Nostrand Reinhold, 1986.

Zelinsky, Marilyn. New Workplaces for New Workstyles. New York: McGraw-Hill, 1997.

Zunz, Olivier. Making America Corporate, 1870–1920. Chicago: Chicago University Press, 1990.

# acknowledgments

This catalog to the exhibition *On the Job: Design and the American Office* is the result of many collaborations, and we would like to recognize those who assisted in its creation.

First we wish to thank M. Arthur Gensler Jr., whose bold vision for this project included a publication from the very beginning. We would also like to acknowledge Diane Hoskins, Kate Kirkpatrick, John Parman, and Belinda Presser at Gensler Architecture, Design & Planning Worldwide for their gracious assistance.

The authors of the four essays, Stanley Abercrombie, Phil Patton, Thomas Hine, and James S. Russell, were accommodating at every turn, and their cooperation made the book a pleasure to produce. Their research and insights not only resulted in these excellent essays, but also aided us in developing the exhibition.

Photo essayist Steven Brooke visually sharpened our perspective on the Dulles High-Tech Corridor, one of the nation's fastest growing office landscapes. National Building Museum Trustees Robert McLean and Julie Rayfield had a direct hand in shaping this visual epilogue. Had it not been for the tour of the Dulles Corridor they organized, the idea for the photographic essay would not have been born. Gratitude also goes to their associates at Cushman & Wakefield and Ai, as well as to Liz Wainger at the Morino Institute.

Research for the project began at NeoCon®1999 World's Trade Fair, the annual conference and exposition for interior design and facilities management professionals held in Chicago's Merchandise Mart. Considering the onslaught of nine hundred exhibitors, it was truly an eye opening baptism by fire. For this introduction, our appreciation goes to Mark Schurman at Herman Miller.

Office furniture manufacturers were most hospitable, and we would like to acknowledge Douglas R. Parker at Steelcase, Mr. Schurman at Herman Miller, and Kristine Vernier at Haworth. They arranged the many tours and meetings with their colleagues that proved extremely useful and enabled us to glimpse behind the scenes. In addition we appreciate the welcome assistance of Apple Computer, Armstrong World Industries, James G. Davis Construction, frogdesign, IDEO, Interface, Johnson Controls, Mannington, SC Johnson, Sun Microsystems, Wilsonart, and all the sponsors of the exhibition.

Grateful appreciation to the numerous institutions, organizations, companies, and individuals who also assisted us in locating images and artifacts. We thank: Christine Cordazzo at Esto Photographics, Henry J. Prebys and Linda Skolarus at the Henry Ford Museum and Greenfield Village, Alden Hathaway at The History Factory, Felicia Looper at Mohawk International, Antiquarian Traders, Richard and Eileen Dubrow Antiques, Chicago Historical Society, Frank Lloyd Wright Foundation and Archives, Hagley Museum and Library, IBM Corporate Archives, Oakland Museum of California, Kevin Roche John Dinkeloo and Associates, Skidmore, Owings & Merrill, Studios Architecture, Winterthur Library, and Xerox Historical Archives.

The Public Museum of Grand Rapids, Michigan, and its permanent exhibition, *The Furniture City*, deserve praise for their insightful look at the industry, history, and people that shaped the city. In Washington, D.C., our colleagues at the Smithsonian Institution's National Museum of American History were extremely helpful and we would like to thank Peter Liebhold, Ann Serio, Carleen Stevens, and William E. Worthington for their time and effort.

For the design of this book and the exhibition, thanks are due to Pentagram Design partner J. Abbott Miller and his associates James Hicks, Jeremy Hoffman, and Roy Brooks. Alicia Yin Cheng provided excellent information graphics. Thanks also go to Laura Latham. Projects such as this would remain incomplete unless fully realized with the intelligence and flair of superb designers, and this is especially true in the case of Abbott.

We are especially indebted to Natalie Shivers, and Elizabeth Johnson, whose exceptional editorial insights helped us clarify our ideas and present them in cogent fashion. This book is published in partnership with Princeton Architectural Press, and we would like to thank publisher Kevin Lippert, project editor Beth Harrison, and adviser Mark Lamster.

At the National Building Museum, we are grateful for the work and support of Martin Moeller, Jennifer Agresta, Zara Anishanslin Bernhardt, Mary Margaret Carr, Terri Cobb, Jan Curtis, Ramee Gentry, Hank Griffith, Lisa Knapp, Michael Kruelle, Essence Newhoff, Christina Wilson, Ed Worthy, and president Susan Henshaw Jones, who artfully guided the project. Special recognition to Museum interns and volunteers Scott Gilbert, Julie Crowe, Emily van Agtmael, Consuelo Angió, Jason McCann, and Mark Howlett.

We would also like to recognize our peers and friends for their counsel and suggestions, including Paola Antonelli, Volker Hartkopf, Edna Johnston, Earl Mark, Reinhold Martin, Carol Willis, and Paolo Polledri, who developed the project in its earliest stages. And finally, thanks to Alan Z. Aiches whose assistance, hospitality, unwavering support, and good humor are especially appreciated.

Donald Albrecht and Chrysanthe B. Broikos
May 2000

# contributors

**Stanley Abercrombie** is an architect, writer, and editor. He has been editor-in-chief of three design magazines including, for fourteen years, *Interior Design*. He was a Loeb Fellow for Advanced Environmental Studies at the Harvard Graduate School of Design where he also taught, and he is a Fellow of the American Academy in Rome, a Fellow of the American Institute of Architects, and an Honorary Fellow of the American Society of Interior Designers. He was the curator of *Industrial Elegance* at the Guggenheim Museum SoHo, and is the author of more than a dozen books about design.

**Donald Albrecht,** co-curator and editor, is an independent curator whose exhibitions include *Stay Cool! Air Conditioning America* and *World War II and the American Dream: How Wartime Building Changed a Nation* (National Building Museum); *National Design Triennial* (Cooper-Hewitt, Smithsonian Institution); and *Making Architecture* (J. Paul Getty Museum). He is exhibition director of the international traveling exhibition *The Work of Charles and Ray Eames: A Legacy of Invention* (Library of Congress and the Vitra Design Museum). Albrecht is also the author of *Designing Dreams: Modern Architecture in the Movies*.

**Chrysanthe B. Broikos,** co-curator and editor, is an architectural historian and curator at the National Building Museum. Her previous projects at the Museum include *Stay Cool! Air Conditioning America*; *The Corner Store*; *El Nuevo Mundo: The Landscape of Latino Los Angeles*; *City Satire: The Illustrations of Roger K. Lewis*; and *Tools as Art IV: Material Illusions* (The Hechinger Collection).

**Steven Brooke** is a noted architectural photographer whose books include *Views of Rome* (winner of the AIA International Book Award), *Views of Jerusalem and the Holy Land, Seaside, The Majesty of Natchez,* and *The Houses of Philip Johnson*. Brooke was awarded the Rome Prize from the American Academy in Rome, the AIA National Institute Honor Award, and two Graham Foundation Grants.

**Thomas Hine** is a writer on culture, history, and design. His books include *Populuxe,* which considered American life and things during the 1950s and 1960s, *The Total Package*, a history and analysis of persuasive containers, and most recently, *The Rise and Fall of the American Teenager: Four Centuries of Being Young*. He was architecture and design critic of the *Philadelphia Inquirer* for twenty-two years, and he writes for many other publications.

**Phil Patton** is the author of several books, including *Made in USA: The Secret Histories of the Things that Made America* (1992) and *Dreamland* (1998). A contributing editor of *I.D.* magazine, *Esquire,* and *Wired,* he also writes frequently about design and technology for the *New York Times*. Mr. Patton was consulting curator for the Museum of Modern Art's 1999 exhibition *Different Roads: Automobiles for the Next Century.*

**James S. Russell** is editor-at-large of *Architectural Record* magazine and regularly contributes articles on architecture and design to the *New York Times*, *Philadelphia Inquirer, I.D.,* the *Harvard Design Magazine,* and *Grid*. He is the principal of WorkDesign, a consulting firm specializing in facilities design that supports advanced workplace management techniques, and teaches at Columbia University's Graduate School of Architecture, Planning, and Preservation. He is a registered architect in New York and a member of the American Institute of Architects.

# index

161

Photograph by Lars Tunbjörk